Saving
Sara

Saving Sara

A Memoir of Food Addiction

Sara Somers

SHE WRITES PRESS

Published 2020
Printed in the United States of America
ISBN: 978-1-63152-846-0 pbk
ISBN: 978-1-63152-847-7 ebk
Library of Congress Control Number: 2019920769

For information, address:
She Writes Press
1569 Solano Ave #546
Berkeley, CA 94707

She Writes Press is a division of SparkPoint Studio, LLC.

Names and identifying characteristics have been changed to protect the
privacy of certain individuals.

To all my GS sisters and brothers who show up abstinent, against all odds, on a daily basis and work to be good, contributing citizens of our planet.

Fear is a natural reaction to moving closer to the truth.

—Pema Chodron

Note to Reader

My primary aim in writing this book is to help people who are compulsive eaters and food addicts, like me.

In this book, I speak about my participation in a twelve-step program for men and women who are recovering from compulsive eating. This program, Greysheeters Anonymous, both saved and transformed my life.

Like Alcoholics Anonymous, this program follows "traditions" that guide the health and integrity of our fellowship. One of these traditions keeps us focused on our main aim: sharing the gift of our program with people who are suffering from food addiction, and who find their way to our program.

Another tradition prevents members from benefiting personally by affiliating themselves with their particular twelve-step program in the media. We don't seek fame or prestige through our participation in our program. In order to follow this tradition to the letter, I could have either used a pseudonym or only my first name, or refrained from stating the name of the program I'm in.

Unlike Alcoholics Anonymous, however, our program is not well known, and has a name that does not make it easy for people to find us when they search for help for compulsive eating or food addiction. Additionally, without using my full name as the author of this book,

I would face significant limitations in terms of making the existence of this book known to potential readers. For these reasons, I have chosen to include the name of the program, and to use *my* real name as well.

To honor the importance and the spirit of our traditions, I affirm that I have no interest in fame or prestige, and I do not represent Greysheeters Anonymous. This is simply my story, which is one among many such stories. I hope that men and women who are being hurt by their relationship with food will, in reading this story, learn that they have the option of benefiting from this life-saving program.

May all compulsive eaters and food addicts find their way to recovery.

Introduction

By age fifteen, I was already thirty pounds overweight. Not only was I fat, I was sullen, and miserable to be with, so much so that my mother threatened to leave me behind when our family moved to Geneva, Switzerland. My father, a professor of political science at Haverford College outside of Philadelphia, was taking his second sabbatical. While he was traveling, which turned out to be 90 percent of the time, my sister, Vicki, and I would live in an apartment with our mother.

A couple of months before we left for Geneva, my mother was sitting in the passenger seat of the family car showing me how the gear shift worked. I was eligible to get my driver's license at sixteen in Pennsylvania and, probably against her better instincts, she'd agreed to teach me how to drive. Her tone and constant exasperation with my dark moods always set me off, and this moment was no exception. As we sat in the car, I screamed at her. I didn't realize it at the time but my mother was as thin-skinned as I was. She reacted immediately. Her only weapon was an ultimatum: "Unless you shape up, we're leaving you behind."

In that moment there was nothing I would rather have than a year without my family. What I really wanted was for nothing to change—to stay in Haverford with my friends.

Like most of her ultimatums, this one didn't hold weight. I went with my family to Geneva, which would only result in more resentment and more gathering proof of all the ways my mother didn't love me. I was full of resentments, anger, and rage, but most of all loneliness. I didn't know what was wrong with me and, like most teenagers, thought I was unique and no one could understand me or would ever try to.

Since the apartment was not ready for us when we arrived, my parents found two rooms in a pension up the main street, Avenue de Chêne, that went into central Geneva. We were three blocks from the International School of Geneva, where Vicki and I were to attend classes.

During that first week in Geneva, we went out to a restaurant that was walking distance from the pension. The restaurant was family-style, a large single room, with straight-backed chairs and no tablecloths on the square tables. After seating us and taking our orders, the waiter brought breadsticks and plopped them on the middle of our table within easy reach of all of us. They were pencil-thin and arrived in a rust–colored glass. I scarfed them down, one by one. I was too busy eating to notice if anyone else wanted or ate any of them.

"Do you think you should be eating all of those?" my father asked me cautiously.

"Leave me alone!" I snapped back at him.

"I'm trying to be helpful."

"I don't want your help."

I kept eating. It was taking forever for our main courses to come. I curled up inside myself and sank deeper and deeper into some dark place that I called my "real self," an imagined self that no one could see but who was thin and loved by everyone. This place I went to in my mind was comforting because I was always right and they were always wrong. In that place, others were punished for not treating me kindly. There was a complete disconnect from that place and the real world, where I alienated everyone, scowling and feeling sorry for myself.

Walking home to the pension that night, my parents argued over my behavior in the restaurant, but I can't remember what was said. I hung back sullenly, provoking my mother even more. If you'd later asked me to describe the lake and my new surroundings, I couldn't have. I was too deep in the Black Hole.

When we got back to the pension, my mother entered the room Vicki and I shared, exploding with frustration and powerlessness. I looked at her and screamed, "You hate me, I know you do!"

She yelled back, "You're right, I do!"

"I knew it, I've always known it."

Out of nowhere, my father's open hand struck my face, causing my nose to bleed.

Vicki rushed between the three of us, yelling, "You're killing her!"

I have an eating disorder. I'm a binger. The episode that unfolded that night in Geneva is a classic incident in the life of a food addict and her family: sullenness, self-centeredness, self-pity at being fat, anger, blaming others, an inability to stop bingeing once certain substances entered my system. In this case, it ended with violence because everyone felt so helpless and powerless. Sometimes it ended with me stalking off, sometimes in bitter silence.

As a family, we never talked about the incident again, though I would pick at the scab and nurse that wound for decades. From iso-lated teenager, I grew into a lonely young woman. The negative inci-dents in my life grew worse. My behavior was unacceptable. I blamed my parents, but anyone was fair game. I treated life like a scoreboard. I tried to convince anyone who would listen just how horrible my parents were. I blamed everything that happened to me on what I'd determined to be my miserable childhood.

Being fat is assumed by most people to stem from a lack of will-power. I think the opposite is true. Fat people exert tremendous will to overcome the prejudices that are heaped on them. Like anyone who starts with a deficit, they have to be better at everything in order to compete in the world. They also have the will to find open stores at any time of the day or night to feed their cravings.

It wasn't until the 1950s that alcoholism was finally accepted as a disease, mental and physical. You can find it in the psychology bible *DSM-5*. I am a food addict, and my disorder is just like alcoholism, but it wouldn't show up in the *DSM* until 1994, and then only as a "non-specified eating disorder."

In May 2013, Binge Eating Disorder (BED) made it into the *DSM-5* as an actual eating disorder diagnosis.[1] I am addicted to sugar, car-bohydrates[2], grains, and volume, which just means more and more of everything. From the time I was eleven or twelve, I always wanted to lose weight. By the time I was in my twenties and thirties and beyond, after years of yo-yoing, years of feeling that I was living in hell, years of the bingeing getting worse and worse, I just wanted to stop killing myself with food. I understood intuitively that my sickness had to do with what I was putting into my body, but I was so fixated on my

---

1   DSM stands for Diagnostic and Statistical Manual of Mental Disorders.

2   In this book, when I refer to carbohydrates or carbs, I'm talking about simple or refined carbohydrates. Carbohydrates are plentiful in vegetables and I eat complex carbohydrates.

weight that I couldn't get past my desire to just be thin and normal like other people I knew, people who ate in moderation.

Throughout my life, I would use food as a solution to everything in an effort to nurture myself as I slid slowly into lonely, dark places where I lived in a complete fantasy world and I was the director of everything that happened to me. Only much later in life would I finally understand that certain foods were the problem. Then there was my attitude, which added to the problem. Tack on hopelessness, and no wonder I was whistling in the dark. In order to find the correct solution, one has to know what the real problem is.

When I was fifteen, in 1963, eating disorders were little understood. A number of books had been published about the dangers of sugar consumption, but what I was suffering from went far beyond that. Not only did I binge excessively, I also exhibited behaviors that are classic symptoms of food addiction: blaming everyone else for my misery, black-and-white thinking, living in anger and rage. I could barely tolerate someone disagreeing with me. If it was a family member, I exploded at them. What people said and what I heard were worlds apart. I was convinced that I was always being criticized. When people opened their mouths, I heard that I was a bad person. One time, after screaming at my mother, using words that weren't allowed in our household, she marched into the bathroom and got soap to wash out my mouth. I thought I saw a razor blade in her hand and was convinced that she intended to cut me. I ran out of the house, terrified. The world I was living in as a young teenager was already far from reality.

Saving Sara is a memoir of food addiction over six decades. It's about my long journey looking for a solution to getting thin. For years, all I wanted was a magic pill that would both eradicate my problems and make me beautiful. What I learned is that there is no such thing. It takes hard work to stop disordered eating behavior. It's easy to quit and give up on ourselves because it's so ingrained in the brain of an addict to treat bingeing as a problem that anyone with enough will-power can deal with. We make promises to ourselves in the morning and are bingeing by evening.

It doesn't help that many consider food addiction "namby-pamby" in comparison to alcohol and drug addiction. Yet counselors in care units say that it is harder to get off sugar than heroin. That is not "namby-pamby."

Until recently, it wasn't understood that an eating disorder was both a physical and a mental illness: an obsession of the mind and the physical cravings set off once the substance is in the body. In my case, the substances were sugar, grains, and refined carbohydrates. I would daydream of being like a Greek hero. I wanted to face my problems like Jason, who met and defeated every challenge until he finally faced Medea to get to the Golden Fleece. But I couldn't get past the first hurdle of not putting sugar and grains in my body—and I emerged from each binge with even more self-hatred than I'd gone in with. I was so filled with dread, terror, and hopelessness that I wanted to die. And yet I was too scared to kill myself. I was living in hell on earth.

If you are a compulsive eater or food addict, if you identify with my story, I hope I can give you one day less of misery. If you are a parent, a teacher, or a professional who works with overweight kids or adults who are obese and difficult to deal with, I hope this gives you some insight into the minds and souls of those who may be afflicted with this disease. They need your love and patience, and they need you to know that they really are in trouble.

As written in my "Note to Readers," I refer here to Alcoholics Anonymous and Greysheeters Anonymous as the two paths that led to my recovery from the insanity of addiction. This book is my story, but it could be about anyone like me. The real story is that there is a solution to the addiction of compulsively eating that is killing people like me.

There may be more than one solution to eating disorders and addictions. This is the one that worked for me. I think of myself as a low-bottom, down-and-dirty eater. I tried almost everything out there; in fact, I can't think of anything I didn't try, except for getting my stomach stapled.

In the appendix of this book, I provide information for getting hold of GSA in the United States and Canada, and also in Europe, Iceland, and Israel.

PART I

*Life is 10% what happens to you
and 90% how you react to it.*
—Charles R. Swindoll

1

I'm Hungry

My cabin at summer camp had two sides open to the elements and two log cabin walls that housed twelve bunk beds. The cabin was tucked under tall, ancient pine trees in the middle of Vermont. I felt close to nature's many voices, comforted by sounds of the wind, the rain pattering on the roofs, the frogs ribbiting in nearby water. I loved everything about camp.

Except for the hiking.

I hated hiking because I couldn't keep up with the rest of the campers. I was nine years old and already twenty pounds overweight. On a nine-year-old girl, that's fat. I was too weak, too fat, and too miserable to hike. I longed to stop and eat as much trail mix as I could shove into my mouth. I was always hungry. Imagine a group of eight nine-year-old girls, packs on their backs, hiking up a trail on Mount Mansfield in Vermont. Seven of those little girls, lithe and energetic, could probably run up the mountain like little goats. Then there's me, always the last girl, lugging up her twenty extra pounds. I am hurting and can barely breathe. The Sarah Bernhardt in me thinks I'm going to die if I take one more step. I fall farther and farther behind the group. The solution to all this, my nine-year-old brain thinks, is to stop and eat a whole bag of trail mix. But I also don't want to get lost, so I keep trudging, doing my best to leave my body by daydreaming my way to the top.

I was clearly different from the rest of the girls. I felt like a Martian among Earthlings. I couldn't connect. I couldn't understand why other girls didn't want to eat all the time and often weren't interested in dessert. How could they stop mid-meal and say they were full? Sometimes it seemed to me that I lived in a glass bell jar: I could see out and others could see in, but it was impossible for me to understand others, and the reverse seemed to be true as well.

One night, I left a roaring campfire where my bunkmates and I were singing camp songs. After telling one of my counselors that I felt sick, I went back to the cabin. When I got there, I saw that someone had put two cookies on each of our beds. The minute I arrived, I gobbled mine down. I spent the next five minutes trying to figure out how I could eat more cookies without stealing them from my cabin mates—or, if I did steal them, how not to get caught. I came up with a plan. I went around to each bed, picked up each cookie, and nibbled in a circle so that each cookie had a significantly smaller circumference. If the teeth marks weren't perfect, I'd go around again trying to make each cookie look normal. I told myself I would get away with it.

Through sheer willpower, I stopped myself from eating all of them. That would be stealing, I told myself.

My bunkmates and our two counselors returned to the cabin thirty minutes later.

"Hey, something's wrong," one of them said. "There are cookies on my bed but they've been chewed on."

"Mine too. That's not fair. What's going on?" added another.

I sat on my bed trying to look innocent. I kept quiet.

"Sara, did anyone else besides you come in the cabin?" one of the counselors, Jane, asked me.

"No. Mine were like that also." Jane looked hard at me. She was trying to decide whether to believe me or not.

The next morning, I told Jane that it was me who'd eaten the cookies. In the future, though, I got much better at living with my lies.

I looked forward to Halloween, my favorite holiday, all year long. When I was old enough to trick or treat without a parent, I would go with friends, always checking their bags to make sure they didn't get more than I did. I would stay out, walking the neighborhood, until the very last moment, pushing my parents' time limits so I could get more and more and more. Once home, I would hoard my stash, telling myself that I would make the candy last. My sister was able to make hers last until Christmas; mine was all gone within twenty-four hours, forty-eight hours at the most. Any time I could find to be alone, I'd rush back to my room and gorge on candy, not tasting anything. I'd come out of my room wondering when I could get back to the bags I had stashed away.

It didn't matter that my parents had rules around sugar consumption. I wasn't trying to rebel; I would have loved to be able to stop the bingeing. But I couldn't. I was scared of the punishment my parents might dole out and I was scared of the bingeing. I felt possessed and didn't know what was wrong with me. Constantly eating sugar is like throwing oil on a fire. I didn't know I was so afraid. What I felt was rage and self-loathing.

"Moderation, Sara," my father used to say to me. But even mentioning the word moderation or suggesting I wait to eat my candy was like poking a rattlesnake with a stick. The venom was out of my mouth before I knew what was happening. And who wanted to live with a rattler? My family walked on eggshells around me. My mother felt completely powerless. Nothing she did or said worked, but she at least had my father to talk to.

My sister, who would struggle with her own eating disorder in her teens, was terrified of me. She had no idea why I was the way I was. She was smaller than me, "right-sized," and there was no other sibling for her to share her fears with.

My mother, who was extremely disciplined, was exasperated by my anger and apparent lack of self-control. I was so hungry for her love and understanding, and I felt helpless and hopeless in my interactions with her.

My father, a professor at Princeton University by the time I was in high school, was the braver of the two. He would make suggestions from time to time, though those never failed to enrage me. If he tried to tell me to pace myself, or that I needed to save room for dinner, I just felt like a failure. My father could debate with politicians and academicians with a healthy sense of humor and a keen intellect, but he was powerless and helpless to help his daughter, whom he truly loved.

My mother confessed to me many years later, well into my adulthood, that she found me intimidating. *What an irony*, I thought to myself. I was totally intimidated by her.

My eating disorder tore up our family just as alcoholism does to families with a practicing alcoholic. I ate all the time. I assumed that the gnawing feeling telling me I had to have more food or I would die was hunger. What I was actually feeling was both physical and mental cravings, but I didn't know either the words or the concept. To me, what I was feeling was hunger; I had to eat and I had to eat NOW. I felt hungry when I was tired, when I was thirsty, when I was angry, and when I experienced almost every other feeling. It was the solution to every discomfort that I had.

Once the obsession hit me, no amount of willpower could stop me. I would eat copious amounts of ice cream or anything else with sugar in it, always falling victim to the cravings. I had to eat until the binge wore itself out. Then I would fall asleep or cry myself to sleep. Eventually, I learned that putting sugar and grains in my body actually triggers the cravings, just like alcohol does for an alcoholic. None of us understood that once I had the sugar in my system, I was powerless over what happened next.

Bingeing in this way is a disease. It destroys families. It leaves a trail of blame, hatred, and sorrow. Everyone loses. It can leave the person who's suffering physically, emotionally, mentally, and spiritually bankrupt, and take the rest of their family right downhill with them. In 1957, alcoholism was just being accepted as a true disease. Anorexia was recognized as a serious disorder by 1952. But bingeing? Back then, we were far from understanding the parallels between food addiction and substance addiction. The very idea that there existed a solution beyond self-discipline to eating too much, to being fat, would have been laughed at. Dieting fads have been popular for 150 years.[3] With the advent of Weight Watchers in 1963 and the steady creation of diet foods, dieting has become a multibillion-dollar business; dieting has slowly become the norm.[4] Yet misunderstanding of obesity and family suffering has only gotten worse. I was one of those who suffered—and my family suffered with me.

3   CBSNews.com, "50 years of Dieting Fads: An American Story"

4   ditto

2

Emotional Hunger

O urs was a typical family of four: my mother and father, my younger sister, Vicki, and me. We also always, it seemed, had two cats. The cats never traveled with us and I have no idea what happened to them each time we moved, but somehow, after every move, we had another two cats. I adored the cats.

My father's family immigrated to the United States from Russia during the first decade of the twentieth century. Daddy was born in Brooklyn, New York, the only one of his family to be born in the States and an American citizen. His entire family—him, his parents, and his two older siblings—lived in a one-bedroom apartment over a grocery store run by my grandmother, Edna. The story that was handed down to me is that my grandfather, Morris, walked the streets of Flatbush in a black bowler hat, discussing philosophy with anyone who would bandy around thoughts on life with him, while Edna ran the store as the sole breadwinner. I never saw a photo of Morris, only my grandmother, a classic-looking, heavy, peasant woman. When my dad's older sister, Aunt Ida, died, people I'd never met came to her funeral and said I looked just like my grandmother. I was about fifty pounds overweight at the time.

When my father was eight or nine years old, people started noticing that he had a beautiful singing voice. From then on, he became the second breadwinner in the family. He was hired out to weddings, birthdays, and anniversaries—anywhere a lovely voice was needed. As an adult, Daddy was stocky, five feet eight inches tall, medium height for a man of his era. He had red hair, so his nickname became "Red." By the time I came along, that was the only name he went by. I inherited his deep worry lines between my eyes. But Daddy's face would relax when he was telling stories. He loved to tell stories and entertain. His students adored him.

Most of the time, I adored him too. He refused to go to bed at night without coming into my bedroom, no matter what my age, no matter what had gone on during the day, and clearing the air. He would say he was sorry for any bad feelings. It's hard not to love a parent who says they're sorry.

He had been a frail baby; surviving his first three years was a major victory. I often looked at photos of him, trying to see that fragile baby, but he always seemed fit and strong to me. Boys growing up in Flatbush lived by their fists, not by their brains. If my dad came home bloody and bruised, his father would ask him, "Did you win?" If the response was no, he'd be sent back out to finish the job. He told me that for a long time, he was headed for a life on the streets and not much good.

The whole direction of his life was turned around when a high school teacher noticed his natural intelligence. Somehow that teacher nurtured that intelligence and managed to foster this budding street fighter's genuine curiosity of life. He went on to the University of Wisconsin as one of a group of Young Turks who all stayed together, graduated together, and moved to Washington DC together. Almost all of them made their mark in American politics. Though my dad did not like talking about his formative years, he never forgot where he came from.

My mother, on the other hand, was an "oops baby" born into a wealthy southern family. She was ten years younger than her next-oldest sibling. Her father was fifty-three years old when she was born, and she told me that he seemed more a grandfather to her than a father. Both her parents were remote. She was raised by a French governess and spoke French before she learned English.

When I was young, I thought my mother looked like a movie star. She was slim, tall, had dark brown hair that she wore in the latest style, and anything she wore looked elegant on her. But by her account she was an ugly duckling growing up—gangly, too tall, awkward.

At thirteen, she was sent away to her aunt Sara's home in Santa Fe, New Mexico, because her eyes had gotten so bad and her face was constantly broken out. Until she was a junior at Vassar College, my mother walked the straight and narrow path, doing what wealthy young women did—attending coming-out parties and joining the daisy chain, Vassar's form of sorority. Her only deviation was that she far preferred Santa Fe and its arty atmosphere to her home in Memphis, Tennessee.

At twenty, while a junior at Vassar, she developed her own mind and started her lifelong journey of working to help people less privileged than she was. She helped create the first workers' union among the dishwashers at Vassar. After she graduated, she joined the International Women's Garment Union. She said her poor mother was always trying to spin a story of her daughter's travels up and down the East Coast that could run in the Society pages of the local paper. My cousin Ellen, nineteen years my senior and a small child when mother was twenty-two, remembers my mother coming home to Memphis after her college graduation, packing up a straw suitcase, and heading off to join the union.

These two unlikely people met on a blind date in 1946 set up by a mutual friend who thought they had such similar minds, they couldn't help but like each other. My father was thirty-five and my mother thirty-three. Both had lived independently for years; my father was in the process of being decommissioned from the army.

Their friend was right. They were married in Santa Fe seven weeks after they met. I came along less than a year later, and Vicki twenty-eight months after me.

I've often wondered if, had she lived in a different time and been encouraged to choose freely, my mother would have had children. She wanted to work all the time. She was passionate about social causes and seemed driven to write about, bring attention to, and better the human living condition. This was a twenty-four-hour-a-day job, and if she could have gone without sleep and food, she would have worked twenty-four hours a day. She hired maids to take care of us, and to clean and cook all our family's meals.

After my sister was born, we moved to Haverford, Pennsylvania where Daddy took a job as chair of the Political Science Department at Haverford College. This was his first job out of Harvard, where he had obtained his PhD. Haverford is located in the western suburbs of Philadelphia. He walked to the campus early in the morning and arrived home in time for dinner. My mother worked at home in a room off the entryway of our rented house. According to her, I was so awful that the first five maids quit. I wanted my mother and was constantly trying to get her attention. I knew she was in the house and could not comprehend why I wasn't allowed to see her. This made her furious. I didn't know what I was doing wrong, and things deteriorated from there.

My father's first sabbatical took us to London in the fall of 1955. He had a fellowship to the London School of Economics.

We lived in a two-room flat with a shared toilet down the hall. I was eight and Vicki was six. The two rooms were tiny and the double bed nearly took up the entire bedroom. Sliding doors separated the bedroom from the living room, but I don't remember them ever being closed. The rooms would have seemed even smaller. The living room couch and its small side table faced a fireplace that required coins in order to function.

I was sent away to boarding school and only came home for holidays. Vicki was sent to a nearby boarding school in London, and got to come home every weekend. My mother told me years later that London was still so war-torn at the time, it was practically impossible to find an affordable apartment for a family of four. Back then, I only knew I was being sent away. I didn't know why, and I hated it.

Vicki was two years and four months younger than me. She was a good baby and grew into a good girl. Whereas I had my mother's brunette hair and brown eyes, Vicki got my father's carrot-red hair and grey eyes. She also had my mother's small, delicate, English bones, while I'd inherited my father's stocky Russian peasant body type. She was cute as a button.

I don't think I ever liked Vicki. I certainly was jealous of her all the time. Before they learned to bring us identical presents when they traveled, my parents would bring each of us something they thought we'd like, and while I took mine I'd be looking at Vicki's. No matter what it was, I wanted it. I would scream in anger until I was given her gift. It was usually Vicki and not my parents who ended my tantrums by giving it to me.

It seemed to my young mind that she did everything right and I did everything wrong. She was sweet and easy to be with and I was just the opposite. My sister got good grades and I didn't. Vicki was athletic and I was fat. She later had boyfriends and wore ID bracelets while I had friends who were boys and told myself that was the best I could have. No one in our family had the courage to face my porcupine personality, to sit me down and explain that life isn't fair—not for me, not for my sister, not for anyone. I wouldn't have believed them if they'd tried to explain this anyway.

When my parents weren't around, I took out all my anger on Vicki. I was mean and hurtful. After one summer when both of us had gone to the same summer camp, it was decided by the camp administrator, in conference with my parents, to keep us separate from then on. It was hard for anyone, camper or counselor, to ignore my cruel behavior toward her. My parents' solution was to send me to camp and let Vicki stay home.

I was eight when we moved to London, and by then I'd determined there was something seriously wrong with me. Clearly I had done something offensive and I was being sent away. I hated boarding school. It was strict and we had to wear uniforms. I cried myself to sleep a lot. I started arguments with other girls about silly things like how to pronounce words such as "cat." With my American accent, I insisted that I was the one who pronounced it correctly—unwinnable arguments. (Ironically, when we returned to the States my mother said I had a perfect posh British accent!)

According to psychologists, if something traumatic happens at a formative age, it will have a profound impact upon the rest of the child's life. I spent years in therapy trying to determine what was wrong with me, and the only thing I was ever able to trace it back to was that year in London. I didn't understand how things were in Europe in the aftermath of World War II. I was encouraged to believe that any loving mother would have refused to live in a place where she couldn't have both her children with her. I felt my resentments were being supported and I dwelled on the past for years.

Back in the States, life to me had become a glass bell jar. I attended Haverford Friends School in the fifth grade. I felt as if could see out and others could see in, but I was unable to connect with anyone. I didn't understand people, and they didn't understand me. I made up stories about their wonderful, loving lives and families. I was steeped in self-pity, which I fed with food and sugar.

I knew something was wrong with me. I was afraid of what it was. So I started a list of "if-onlys" that grew as the years went by:

If only I had a different mother, I wouldn't be fat and feel so lonely.

If only we didn't move all the time, I'd have better friends.

If only I was thin, I'd be more popular.

If only I was blond, I'd be thinner.

If only the adults would leave me alone, I'd be happier.

I convinced myself that I knew what the problem was (see above list), and I was sure I knew the impossible answers. None of the problems went away, though, so my solutions remained fantasies in my head, where they took up a lot of space. I was unable to concentrate in school and my grades were barely passing ones.

My parents began their own litany:

"You have such a pretty face; if only you could discipline yourself better and not eat so much."

"You are so intelligent; why can't you get better grades?"

They were beyond frustrated. I would understand that much later, but when they tried punishing me it only enraged me more. And Vicki was the outlet for all my anger, hopelessness, and sense of failure. I lashed out at her physically when my anger reached volcanic proportions. I don't remember hitting her, but Vicki says I did.

The angrier I was, the more my family distanced themselves from me. Eventually, I developed a firm position about my place in the family: no one cared about me, so why should I care about anyone else?

3
I Just Want to Belong

By the time I graduated high school, I had been to thirteen schools and lived in five different states and three different countries. No one in my small young world moved as much as we did. In first grade, my parents registered me at Haverford Friends, and then they decided that Bryn Mawr Primary was a better school and moved me there a few weeks into September. Two years later, two weeks into third grade, I was taken out of Bryn Mawr and we boarded the Queen Mary and went to England for the year.

I started out at one boarding school south of London but was so miserable after five months there that my parents took me out and enrolled me in a different one. At the end of that year, back we went on the Queen Mary, and by the end of August we were living in Kensington, California, and I was enrolled in the primary school there.

After teaching for the year at UC Berkeley, my father found he missed working at a small campus, so the following year we were back in Haverford and I was a student at Haverford Friends once again. I was ten years old and, counting nursery school and kindergarten, had already attended eight schools. I was fat (and getting fatter), self-conscious, and had no confidence that I'd be liked. The harder I worked at being liked, the harder it got. I just wanted to belong.

I had no sense of belonging in my family. Somewhere in my first decade, I'd convinced myself that I was adopted and my parents thought they'd made a huge mistake and that was why no one in my family liked me. Ice cream gave me temporary relief from the many miseries that were building up. So did my revenge fantasies: *Just wait till I grow up, I'm going to show you. You'll be sorry you were so mean to me.*

I envied all those kids who never moved. Living inside my layers of fat, I wasn't able to just observe. I saw what was different and jumped to conclusions that fit neatly on my checklist of everything that was unjust in my life. It seemed to me that the kids I wanted to hang out with came from a different species of family—a species that stayed put, that surrounded their young with love and support until they were old enough to venture out on their own.

Those parents were at least a decade younger than my parents. They didn't seem to put work in front of caring for their children. My academically ambitious parents wanted to change the world, make it a better place to live in, but couldn't seem to identify my growing desperation for what it was and instead always saw my behavior as acting out.

Parenting clearly wasn't a priority for my parents. Both of them were highly intelligent. Many called my father brilliant, and he loved teaching. My mother was driven to work. She was writing and doing research. When she was absorbed in her work, no one was to disturb her for anything, for any reason—but I couldn't, or chose not to, remember that rule. I would constantly knock on her door, only to be greeted with a "What now?" The needier I got, the more pissed off she got.

My father would tell me two stories when I was in my twenties. The first was that when I was under a year old and still couldn't walk, he would—at the request of my mother, who had bursitis in her elbow—put me in my crib in the morning before he left for work. My mother couldn't lift me and probably didn't spend much time with me. "You would spend as much as eight hours a day in your crib," he told me. "You didn't get any exercise, and I'm sure it added to your plumpness."

One evening, when they were playing bridge with friends, I started crying.

"I jumped up and was going to get you out of the crib and walk around with you," my dad said. "The women who were there stopped me and told me I'd just be spoiling you." He looked very sad. "I've never forgiven myself."

It was as if he were admitting to me in the telling of that story, "You are right, we weren't good parents." I was grateful to have my long-held negative feelings confirmed, but it was too little too late. The damage had been done. I didn't know what it felt like to be held and hugged when I cried. I never felt a part of our family. It meant something that he was willing to tell me the story, but at twenty-four years old, I wasn't able to forgive my parents. In my mind, they were the cause of all my many problems.

The second story he told me was about something that happened when I was two or three years old. He used to walk the twenty to thirty minutes from our house to his office on campus. He would walk down Panmure Road, the street we lived on, that wasn't used much except by the families who lived there. Then he'd turn left onto Railroad Avenue, a busy street that took him to the boundary of the campus. Then he'd turn off and cut through some woods, pass the Duck Pond, and arrive at his office.

"One morning, as I was walking on Railroad Avenue, I heard crying behind me. I turned around and there you were, in the middle of the street following after me." He shook his head in wonder. "I don't know how you got out of the house. I don't know how you stayed safe, but my heart nearly stopped. You must have been behind me for five or ten minutes. I grabbed you up and we went home." He paused. "I don't think your mother noticed you were gone."

I'm sure my father thought that if only he'd done things differently, I wouldn't have suffered the way I did. It's hard to know. No one had ever even heard of food addiction at the time. To them I was just an undisciplined, out-of-control, needy child who wouldn't obey any rules. I was a huge annoyance. I was in trouble a lot. I was alone a lot. I cried a lot, and I ate a lot.

Bad parenting didn't cause my illness, but it made life hell for me and deepened the hole of emptiness inside of me. I couldn't have named it as being suicidal at the time, but in retrospect I would see it as that. I certainly wanted to disappear, and on extreme days I wanted to die. I don't remember feeling differently, except at rare moments. Yet a part of me was determined to find ways of taking care of the hurt inside.

My mother, sister, and I belonged to the Ardmore Skating rink, a prestigious ice rink where Olympic athletes trained. It was a popular place for adults and kids on the Main Line. Walking in the front doors, a friendly, familiar brisk chill would wake my face up, and then the canned music that filled the whole rink would surround me. Teens of all ages came in the afternoons and skated counter-clockwise on the ice. The talented skaters were in the middle or at the far end, practicing difficult jumps.

My friends and I would rush straight for the locker rooms, passing the snack bar on the right as we ran by. Putting on our skates, we talked about the latest 45s and when we were going to buy them. Then we got on the ice.

I loved skating but I was too heavy to compete. I had excellent balance and when I skated I could sway to the music. Moving on the ice, I didn't feel heavy or dumpy. I was a good skater. I knew it, and it made me happy. I would dream that my mother was there watching and could see that I did something well. The time always flew by. After an hour, the ice machine came out to clean the ice, and everyone had to leave the rink for five or ten minutes. My friends would use the break to buy something in the snack bar. I wasn't allowed to spend money there, so I reluctantly just hung around the edges of the ice, waiting for them to come back out, waiting to get back on the ice.

One day, when I was eleven or twelve years old, I saw a quarter on the ice. With my heart pounding, I grabbed it and looked to see if anyone near me had dropped it. When no one claimed it, I dashed into the snack bar and handed over my quarter for five five-cent candy bars.

As I held the candy, I felt a rush so powerful it was intoxicating. I had found a way to get sugar without going through my parents. Instinctively, I knew I had to figure out how to keep this feeling going, a way I could get my sugar fixes on my own. I had to find a means to get money. I wasn't even a teenager and already I was thinking like the addict I was becoming.

That one quarter changed my life. After that, my parents no longer had control over me. I started taking coins from my mother's purse. I was furtive about it. I snuck around the house, trying to locate where she had put her purse. I always found it.

Time passed and coins stopped being enough. I started taking dollar bills. My mother never said a word about any money going missing, and I thought I was invincible. I started taking two dollars at a time. The thrill of getting away with something, but seemingly invisible, filled me with a sense of power and confidence I'd never known. I wasn't careless about it. I only stole once or twice a month, and I always spent it on candy that I ate outside the house.

A year went by and I went for bigger stakes: I stole a five-dollar bill. That night, my mother came into the living room and accused me, to my face, of taking her money.

I was sitting on the couch with my sister and father, who was reading to us, when my mother entered the room.

"There is five dollars missing from my wallet, and I think you took it," she said, looking at me.

"I didn't do it." I was scared but brazen.

"I think you did."

"You can think what you want."

"I want to see your coin purse this minute."

I burst into tears. "You never believe me about anything."

Then I ran out of the room.

Lying was coming easily to me. I had learned in the first grade that no one believed me anyway. That year, a student had stolen something from another student's desk. Convinced it was me, the teacher and then the principal had grilled me. I remembered well standing outside the classroom, the door wide open, being endlessly drilled. When that didn't work, they tried the soft touch: "You'll feel so much better if you just tell us the truth." I was crying and scared and begging them to believe me, but they didn't.

Some weeks later, they discovered the culprit. My teacher made a weak apology. I didn't feel vindicated.

I backed off stealing from my mother after her accusation, but I didn't stop completely. And then, at thirteen, I got caught red-handed. We had moved away from Panmure Road and were living in a more modest place on the north end of the campus. Across the very busy street was an A&P grocery store. I often spent lonely afternoons on the weekends, avoiding homework, daydreaming yet bored with myself. Wanting some excitement, I went out, crossed the street, and walked into the A&P. I had nothing in mind, and I had no money, so I was just wandering. Then I came upon the magazine rack with all the teen magazines. Each one had covers of pretty, slim young girls who were wearing clothes I wanted. Next to the photos were promises and suggestions: *How to get your boyfriend to like you better.* Well, I had to get a boyfriend first. *How to dress like Annette Funicello.* Mesmerizing! I had to have one.

I didn't think anything out; I just rolled one up, put it in the back of my skirt, and walked out the door.

Five minutes later, I was lying on my bed, drinking in the important information that was going to make me a different person, when my mother burst into my bedroom.

"There is a man downstairs who says you took a magazine from the A&P," she said.

I couldn't lie; the magazine was in my hands. She got that look on her face that said she was fuming. If I pushed it, she'd double my punishment.

"Take that magazine back right now, apologize, and pay for it."

I had to walk across the street, following the A&P guy. I felt fifty pairs of eyes watching my walk of shame. I wasn't really sorry I had stolen. I was sorry I'd gotten caught.

I handed the cashier the dollar from my allowance, and they let me go with a warning. I wanted to be anyone other than who I was.

The warning scared me, and I didn't steal again after that for a couple of years. Meanwhile, we moved to Geneva for a year and then the following year, instead of moving back to Haverford, to Princeton, New Jersey. The college had made my dad an offer he couldn't resist. Besides other perks, they were willing to pay one half of both my sister's and my college education.

New school, new friends, new start. Maybe I could be someone other than me. I managed to lose some weight by eating 500 calories a day (my first diet), and my grades went up as I was now in public school and had spent the previous four years in private schools. But I still lived with my family, and I still had something inside of me that said what I had wasn't enough—that *I* wasn't enough.

I got my driver's license, but unlike my friends, who just had to pay for gas, my dad sat me down for a serious conversation.

"Cars are expensive to run. It's not just gas," he told me. "I want you to understand that." And he proceeded to break down how much everything cost. By his estimation, our VW bug cost eleven cents a mile to run (this was 1963).

"I want you to keep a notebook in the car and write down the mileage when you leave and again when you get home. We'll add it up at the end of each month, and you can pay four cents a mile."

This wasn't negotiable.

I was infuriated. Once again, they were making me different. I was going to show them. Some smart "bad boy" told me that it was easy to disconnect the line to the odometer on a VW. He took me to the car, opened the front trunk cover, and showed me the line and exactly how to do it. I was thrilled. Having this information opened up a world of driving to me. I would sneak out my bedroom window at night, steal the car, roll it down our hill, undo the odometer, and then drive. Just drive. Out on country roads by myself. I loved driving. I never wanted to be in the passenger seat.

I don't think my parents ever found out about my nighttime escapades. If they did, they didn't tell me. The truth was that everyone walked on eggshells around me. Both my parents are now dead but it wouldn't surprise me to learn they knew a lot more than I realized but put off confronting me. Life was miserable enough in our house without creating guaranteed fights. But as my "criminal" behavior increased, their lack of confrontation led me to believe that these behaviors were invisible. That I was way smarter than the grown-ups.

In Princeton, my mother would take me to Kresge's Company for new clothes in the fall. No way was I going to wear those clothes when friends were wearing Villager outfits and Papagallo shoes. Clothes were extremely important to us. We were at an age where we all wanted to wear similar things. So I threw another brick on my mountain of resentments and took matters into my own hands.

There was a department store called Bambergers in Princeton that I frequented. I may have started by stealing something small, like a belt, but I went for the big time fairly quickly. One day I went in and scooped up four or five dresses I liked. When no saleslady was looking, I took the dresses to the dressing room, put one on after the other, and put my own dress back on—since I was larger than most kids my age, this didn't look odd on me. I, then, nonchalantly sashayed out of the store. I didn't get caught. I was sixteen, and I thought I had *it*—whatever it took to be brave enough to walk in and walk out without raising suspicion. I got high on my own derring-do. I wasn't drinking yet, but I was intoxicated by my own power to get away with things.

With food, with clothes, with money, I always wanted MORE. If I got something I thought I wanted, I'd be happy for five minutes and then my mind would want bigger, better, ten of them. I was obsessed with MORE. Bingeing was compulsive. I would have a thought that I was hungry and start eating, and then I couldn't stop. With money, it was a means to what I perceived as an end—buying food I wasn't supposed to eat. I had no on/off button. I was completely unable to say or act upon "enough." There was never enough. Never. As long as I wasn't getting caught, I thought I was slick and cool.

It would be years before I made the connection that the obsessive quest for MORE, the bottomless hole inside of me that kept insisting that nothing was ever enough, and all the bad behavior involved trying to meet those insane ideas, was causing a deep depression, an inability to focus in school or on much else, and even feeling suicidal because I was powerless and thought that this was all someone else's fault.

In my mind, I was a poor, helpless victim and the world owed me.

4
Hiding In and Out of the Closet

B y the time I was fifteen years old, there was no doubt in my mind that something was drastically wrong with me. I thought it was the family I'd been born into. I thought eating was the solution to my misery, even though it was obvious to everyone else that the way I thought about food and was gaining weight wasn't normal. I didn't want anyone to see or to know what I was doing. I was too ashamed to admit what I was doing. I wanted to be cured of suffering, cured of my weight problems, but I didn't want any suggestions from anyone. My emotional state of being was a roller coaster. I might have been diagnosed as bipolar, my swings were so dramatic. But I wasn't bipolar. I was a food addict.

I had moments of joy that made me high, followed by deep depressions. I was either stealing five dresses at a time or being angelically good. The word "moderation" did not exist for me. I knew the definition of the word but when my father would helplessly watch me scarfing down food and offer, "Can you try and eat in moderation?" the answer was no. I was completely incapable. The shame made it impossible for me to admit to him that I felt powerless, that I was scared and felt hopeless. I didn't want him saying anything to me, reminding me of that powerlessness. So, I began my eating/bingeing in secret—at least, I thought I did.

Bingeing is an intimate act, which is one of the ways it's a different kind of addiction from alcoholism. Alcoholics can succumb to their addiction at bars and be considered the life of the party. The beginning stages of alcoholism are socially acceptable. Food addicts, on the other hand, always binge alone. The act of bingeing is both compulsive and shameful. Even in the midst of a binge, we are trying with every ounce of willpower not to binge.

As my bingeing progressed, I would often be sitting on the floor in front of the fridge, or on my bed surrounded by cookie crumbs, crying my eyes out, while compulsively continuing to binge. I desperately wanted things to be different. I wanted to be well, not to be engaging in these behaviors, and yet I couldn't stop. If you think this sounds a lot like insanity, you're right. It is definitely a type of insanity.

My family loved ice cream. My mother would buy it in half-gallon rectangular boxes. There was always a box of coffee, a box of vanilla, and often the triumvirate of vanilla, chocolate, and strawberry in the freezer. After our family dinner, one parent would serve each of us a single helping for dessert—but that was never ever enough for me.

Wanting more doesn't accurately describe the single-minded obsession of the addict—of wanting what you want *now*—or how that can drive your whole evening. In our split-level home, my bedroom was a half floor below the kitchen, whereas my parents' and my sister's bedrooms were a half floor above. Down in my room, I'd wait impatiently, supposedly doing homework, until it seemed to me that all was quiet in the kitchen. Then I'd sneak back up, go to the freezer, and retrieve the half-gallon carton of ice cream. Standing in front of the freezer, often with the door still open, I'd grab a spoon, open the opposite end from the one already opened, and eat as much and as fast as I could. *That's all I want*, I'd tell myself, as if I had some control over the quantity. I'd really mean it at the moment I thought it, even though I hadn't tasted anything and it had not been satisfying at all. I ate so fast that I often got brain freeze. Then I'd hold my head under the faucet, lapping up warm water until my head stopped hurting.

This all took place in less than five minutes. All the while, I was in a state of intense anxiety, wondering if my parents would hear me and come investigate what was going on. I'd creep back down to my room, returning to my homework that I hadn't started. But it was impossible to focus when all I was thinking about was the ice cream in the freezer, calling my name. I might hold out for as much as fifteen minutes but then I'd be sneaking back upstairs to the freezer and doing it all over again. Eating fast and furious, getting brain freeze, running warm water, gulping it down, and escaping back downstairs before my parents were any the wiser.

This repeated itself until I realized that there was only half an inch of ice cream between my binge side and the side that had been opened for the family. Then, with great effort and even greater fear of the consequences, I left the ice cream box as it was.

Nobody ever said a word to me about the food that disappeared. Just as with the car and my night driving, I thought I was getting away with something. I know I terrorized my parents and my sister. I know I made it impossible for anyone to talk to me. I had to have the last word. I screamed in rage if I thought one or the other parent was picking on me. I wouldn't hesitate to lie, even when the truth was obvious. I'd slam doors and lock myself in my room.

I didn't have a clue what was wrong. If my dad suggested it might be lack of willpower, I flew off the handle. Everything he said that he thought might be helpful only served to bring to my attention the fact that my behavior felt completely out of my control. I hated myself and I hated everyone in my family who made me aware of my powerlessness. My home was a constant battleground. There were no words at that time for families that lived with and survived an active addict, but I'm sure all four of us were suffering from PTSD by the time I graduated high school.

The summer before my junior year of high school, I managed to lose twenty-five pounds. I was sixteen years old and we had just moved to Princeton, New Jersey. A new city, a new high school, a new me! We lived twenty minutes' walking distance from Princeton High School. Just thinking about going to high school set my heart aflutter. I wanted the life I'd seen in *Teen* magazine. I wanted an Ozzie and Harriet family—a home where our life revolved around our escapades and family togetherness. I wanted that kind of attention and belief in a world where no matter what happened, everyone loved each other, and everything would work out.

Within six weeks of the new academic year, I started dating my first-ever boyfriend, Bob. I adored him. He was handsome, with sandy-colored hair and a pleasant but unremarkable face. He was on the football team and bigger than me. I felt normal-size standing next to him. We spent all our time together, and I kept my weight off. I thought I was pretty hot stuff. My grades soared. Because of private school and the International School of Geneva, I was academically ahead of my fellow classmates. I developed confidence for the first time in my life. I was popular. No one had ever seen me weighing 175 pounds. No one knew me as the girl who slunk through the school halls wanting to be both invisible and loved by everyone at the same time. None of my new friends had ever experienced my depressions and constant anxiety. I was close to right size, I had a boyfriend, and I was liked.

The better I did in school, the more motivated I became to study and get good grades. I made the honor roll for the first time, and my reward was that I was allowed, if I wanted, to watch one hour of TV on weekday nights. I woke up on time and thought about what I would wear. I learned to sew and made cool clothes so I didn't have to wear what my mother bought at Kresge's. Bob would meet me en route to school each morning. His last name also started with S, so we had the same homeroom. I started to feel normal. I started to believe that my problems were finally over.

For a year and a half, I no more understood how I was keeping the weight off than I'd understood in the past how the bingeing had grabbed me by the throat. It felt like magic. I had no ability to be self-reflective. To my sixteen-year-old mind, the gods of Greek myths I had studied in school were finally smiling on me. Like every teenager, I lived in the moment. I was happy, and I felt that as long as I didn't change anything, nothing would change. In spite of my crappy family, things were going to get better.

One night during the spring of my junior year, Bob came to dinner to meet my family. My mother had inherited old mahogany furniture from her mother, and our small living room/dining room area was full of the dark, heavy, late nineteenth-century furniture. Our house seemed sad even during the day. At the oval dining room table, my sister always sat on the side closest to the kitchen, and I sat opposite her. My mother sat to my right and my father to my left. This never changed unless someone wasn't home. That night, Vicki was having a sleepover at a friend's house. While we were eating and I was trying extremely hard to be nice, conversational, and a good daughter, I caught my mother staring at me.

"Someday you are going to be a raging beauty," she said, apropos of nothing.

Without skipping a beat, my father said, "Right now she's just raging."

I don't think he meant to humiliate me in front of Bob, but that is exactly where I went. For the first time in years, maybe ever, my mother had given me an unsolicited compliment, and just as quickly my father had taken it away. I couldn't win. I felt as if I'd been slapped, hard, and I went numb. I didn't do or say anything, just kept sitting there while the hurt joined all the other past hurts that had been festering inside of me.

"Did you like Bob?" I asked my mother the next day.

Bob was shy and quiet. His father was a salesman and his mom was a stay-at-home mother. To me, they were the normal family that I wanted. They liked me, and I liked them. Bob really liked me. We told each other all the time that we loved each other. He listened to me and was empathetic if I complained about my family.

I waited hopefully. I really wanted her to be happy for me.

"Well, he's nice but you could do better."

"What do you mean? He's wonderful."

"You asked me. I'm telling you. He doesn't seem to have any ambition. You're smarter than he is. I don't think he'll go anywhere in life."

I was stunned. I had gone to her with an open, happy heart. It didn't occur to me to protect myself or be on guard. I wanted her approval. She might as well have punched me in the belly. I was without words. I just stared at her, unable to defend him or do much of anything.

It was a short conversation that had a huge impact. Within weeks, I broke up with Bob. I had no reason. Nothing was wrong. But my mother had flipped the switch that said "BETTER/MORE," and just that quickly I was thinking he wasn't enough—not good enough, not smart enough.

At first, I was fine with my new status. I had dates with a few other boys. But they weren't Bob and I started to miss him. My pride wouldn't let me tell him I'd made a mistake. In fact, I was nasty to him whenever I saw him, as if it were his fault we were no longer together.

This became a dating/relationship pattern for me. Every couple of years, I would lose weight. I would find a boyfriend who matched up with my low self-esteem (with two exceptions), start feeling superior, dump the boyfriend because he didn't meet my (my mother's) expectations, and then grieve the relationship as if I was the victim. Inevitably, while wallowing in victim mode, I'd gain back all my weight, plus more. Nothing was ever enough—not enough food, not enough love, not enough character. It didn't really matter what it was. I was never satisfied.

After two years of high school in Princeton, I graduated. I had been accepted to Lake Forest, a small college in the northern suburbs of Chicago. I'd hated filling out college applications. My father and I had battle after battle because he wouldn't let me do something fun until I'd written the essay required of each application. I wanted it to be easy. I wanted to smile at someone and have them open their arms wide and say, "Oh yes, we want you at our institution." I hated HARD. I hated the word. I hated the concept of working diligently to accomplish something.

As graduation got closer, all the changes—breaking up with Bob, the end of high school, leaving friends—began to penetrate my mind and I started bingeing again. Once more, I was at the mercy of my addiction, with no comprehension as to why any of this was happening to me. I was short-tempered and had the attention span of a flea. Just like everyone else in my life had done, I thought the gods had abandoned me.

I was actively bingeing when I was hired as an au pair by a
Princeton family for the summer before my freshman year of college.
I had dressed carefully for my interview and, like an actor, put on
the best possible face, never mentioning any fears I might have with
so much responsibility. I was to care for two boys under six and live
with the family in their summer home in the Adirondack Mountains
of upstate New York.

I couldn't care for myself, much less two small children. I was a
terrible babysitter. The times that I was asked to sit for an evening, I
ate everything I could get my hands on. My parents told me to wash
any dishes the family may have left in the sink, and maybe I'd be
asked back.

I didn't realize then how very forgiving those families were.
Surely they were disturbed to have found out that their babysitter,
instead of just indulging in a snack, had eaten all of their ice cream
and cookies, wiping them clean of any desserts they might have had
in the house.

During that summer in the Adirondacks, I ate and I binged. I lay
on the couch reading "deep" books. I was lazy and only did things
when I was asked to. The mother, Mrs. X, was already worried about
me before we had even left Princeton, but for the wrong reason—my
large breasts. (Someone told an au pair I met at the swimming pool
this.) I suppose she thought this meant that I would attract the attention of boys.

Mrs. X was severe-looking, not very tall, dark, and clearly the
boss of the family. The family's Adirondack home was owned by her
mother, who also spent the summer next door. Mrs. X was the only
woman in her nuclear family, and she set the tone and the rules.

The weeks went by in a blur, a drunken haze in which little survives in my memory until the final week of my stint with them. Up
until that point, Mrs. X had kept her thoughts and opinions about
me to herself. She was firm, unsmiling, and, I thought—probably

correctly—didn't much like me. During that last week, she took me aside. "I think we should have a talk, evaluate your summer."

I was holding my breath.

"This was not a success," she said. "You didn't seem to like being here. You slept a lot and it seemed you were always reading. I had to ask you to do things that you should have thought of yourself. Didn't you like us, the kids?"

"I'm sorry."

"That's not good enough, Sara. It's like you don't know how to be part of a family. You kept yourself apart the entire summer." She wasn't being unkind, just straightforward—something I wasn't used to. "I'm not going to insult you by making excuses for you but I hope you think long and hard before signing on as an au pair again."

I was crying as she told me what an au pair in a family does. "I know you're right. We aren't close in my family. I don't think my mother likes me." And I really sobbed. She was kind enough to listen to me, and maybe she had some empathy. But it was clear I was not invisible to her.

I thanked her and meant it when we finished. I had never felt more cared for in my life than I did in that hour she spent confronting me. I knew instinctively that she had given me a gift. *You are visible,* she was saying to me. *What you do and don't do has an impact on everyone around you.* It was the first but not last time I'd be given this kind of feedback.

There are people who, once they are given constructive feedback or have an insight about themselves, are able to start making behavioral changes to improve their lives. Addicts can't do that. The disease is so much more powerful than the knowing. When I got the compulsion to eat or a knee-jerk reaction to rage at someone, everything I knew went out the window. I was like an amnesiac. The compelling drive to satisfy the craving, to give into fear or anger, was the only thing that existed in the moment for me. After the binge ran its course, when the damage from my anger was done, only then would I remember that I was going to do something different the next time. But it was too late. Those precious moments when someone courageously mirrored back to me what my behavior was doing were completely lost, stored in some attic in my mind for exploration years later.

5
Leaving the Nest

I began my freshman year at Lake Forest College in the fall of 1965. Lake Forest is on the western shore of Lake Michigan, halfway between Chicago and Wisconsin. It is a beautiful, small suburban town, home to very wealthy families. The streets are wide and quiet and have old, leafy green trees lining the sidewalks. Even in winter, when all the trees have lost their leaves, it's stunningly beautiful.

The year before I arrived, there was an ice storm. When I got to school, I saw photographs of what it had looked like during the storm. The town could have been an ice sculpture; the photos underscored the town's majestic beauty.

The buildings on the campus reflected the old money present in town. My dormitory, a lovely building originally built in the early 1900s, was three stories and had twelve rooms on each floor. My room was like any other freshman room: two twin beds, two desks, two chests of drawers, and a communal bathroom down the hall.

In 1965, LFC functioned as if it was still the 1950s. Girls and boys were separated by gender and the rules around comingling were strict. By the time I graduated in 1969, less than four years later, most of the dorms were coed and the rules had become extremely lax. LFC was tripping into the hippie years of the 1970s.

On my arrival, the first thing I was handed was a green and white beanie. Wanting to belong, I put it on my head, but as soon as my new roommate, Dorothy, walked into our shared space, she took one look at me in my beanie, turned on her heel, and walked out. I must have looked ridiculous, and I imagine she dismissed me as some teenybopper—but her first impression couldn't have been more off the mark. Over time, she'd put up with a lot from me.

Dorothy wasn't a sorority type. She was a tall, lean girl from Louisville, Kentucky, and she was a bit of a loner herself. She cared about her studies, and she took care of herself. When I think of her, I picture her looking at me with her head slightly cocked, one eyebrow raised, and a skeptical look on her face. She seemed to find my "search for meaning"—the late nights smoking and writing painful poetry—somewhat amusing. I had never lived so close to someone around the clock. I felt exposed and needed thicker walls around my emotions. She kept her own counsel and didn't show her reactions to my swings of energy, my constant need for music in the room, my depressions, and my sinking grades, which I pretended to be unaffected by.

Freshman year was hard, more challenging than I could ever have predicted. Freshman classes seemed always to be scheduled at the worst hours. I would stay awake late into the night reveling in my new "freedom," and then regularly sleep through my 8:00 a.m. classes. Often, I slept until noon, jeopardizing my grades and even risking flunking out.

I had learned no self-discipline in high school, only how to rebel against authority. Now that I was in college, I was on my own. It was strange, and my lack of self-care skills was obvious. I started smoking. I started drinking coffee for the first time in my life. I longed for the life of a beatnik. I would skip meals, thinking, *I can control my food intake.* Then I'd hit the vending machines with a vengeance.

When you're addicted to sugar, bingeing is energizing. It can be difficult to sleep or even calm down internally. Then, when the sugar high wears off, you drop like a rock in a pond and become depressed—but it's still hard to sleep. I began reading depressing books in an attempt to identify with someone or something. Dorothy, who kept regular hours for the most part, was stupefied by my behavior. I was pushing every limit I had. And I was unhappy.

My father came to visit me one weekend and we got into a conversation about freedom as we walked around campus.

"I can do whatever I want here," I told him. "I'm totally free. I don't have to go to classes. I can stay awake all night."

"If you don't have any boundaries, you aren't free, Sara," he said, shaking his head. "What you are calling freedom is a trap."

I looked at him as if he were speaking Chinese. I argued with him rather than take in any advice. I defended my low grades. "I don't care as long as I'm passing," I said.

I was lying. I cared very much.

He stopped walking and looked at me. "If you want a B, you aim for an A. Always aim above what you think you want."

He spoke to me as if I had the maturity and wherewithal to take this in. He was forgetting, or he refused to realize, that his eighteen-year-old daughter had no maturity and no ability to assimilate his wisdom.

On nights I couldn't sleep, I'd read until early dawn. One pre-dawn morning, I stayed awake to finish *I Never Promised You a Rose Garden*, by Joanne Greenberg, a story about a young girl who is institutionalized for mental problems. She is very troubled and ends up getting much-needed help by the end of the novel.

I wanted help. I thought her story was romantic. In the book, she burns the soft insides of her arms with a cigarette; I decided to mimic that craziness. I wanted to know exactly how she felt. So I took a lit cigarette and held it to my skin just above my left wrist.

The cigarette burned a round hole in my arm in the same place a watch face would be. It didn't hurt, not even when my skin turned white.

That night, in the dark, just before the dawn, I saw my wound as a badge of courage. But when I woke up hours later, some sanity had set in and I was deeply ashamed that I would even contemplate hurting myself like that. For years, I never told anyone what I had done, and I wore a watch all the time to cover the scar.

Before I began college, my father had sat me down to tell me how my four years were going to work financially. Princeton University was paying about 50 percent of my tuition. For my freshman year, my father would pay the other 50 percent. My sophomore year, he would pay 35 percent. His percentage would get lower each succeeding year and mine would get higher. This was not negotiable. I had to get a job, show up on time, be responsible, make money, and invest in my own education.

I didn't know how to do this, and beyond that, what he was asking me to do didn't appeal to me. It was spring of freshman year, and I had to find a job that summer. The only thing I'd ever known or done during the summer was go to summer camp or be in the Adirondacks. Being an au pair was out of the question, so I wrote to the director of the camp I'd attended as a girl and inquired if there might be a job for me as a counselor. Maybe because I had been a camper since I was nine years old, or maybe because my family was Quaker and the camp was run on Quaker principles, she took a chance on me and I landed a summer job.

It was as if I'd never heard a word of Mrs. X's feedback from the summer before. I was completely irresponsible, wandering off at all times of the day by myself, daydreaming, and letting others shoulder my responsibilities. I also stole ice cream from the kitchen late at night with my best friend, Tami. We didn't get caught, but our head counselors likely knew. We'd stand in front of the huge camp freezer, shoveling ice cream into our mouths, and I'd proudly tell Tami about all my ice cream theft escapades back at home. Because she did the stealing with me, that somehow made it legitimate. I wasn't hiding in the shadows, hoping my parents wouldn't walk in on me. I was having fun with my best friend at summer camp.

I lived my life vicariously through Tami. She was pretty, with curly, dark hair that framed her pixie face. She was slim and wore a cream Irish knit fisherman's sweater in the evenings when it got cool. I wanted a sweater like hers so badly. I was sure boys would pay more attention to me if I had one, because then I'd look like Tami. The counselors at the boys' camp adored her. Listening to her relate her dates with guys, I daydreamed of being thin, of my life being different, better, full of people who loved me. I used every occasion I could find to sit by water or under a tree and "contemplate." I created a life in my head: I would become a starving artist or writer, and all this pain and angst would be grist for the artistic mill.

I was the junior counselor in a cabin with eight eleven-year-old girls and a senior counselor. She and I were charged with the girls' welfare for a large part of the day. I cared much more that the girls adored me than about teaming up with my co-counselor and setting a good example. Once more, I found myself in a position of being paid to care for others and not being able to care for myself. I only thought about what would make me happy *now*, in the moment. I had no capacity to step outside of myself and wonder what might make someone else happy.

And yet, my summers in Vermont had instilled in me some respect for the natural world. As a camper, I had helped build some of the cabins onsite. I'd installed logs for stairs going from the waterfront up to the main lodge. I had learned to swim in the lake and paddle a canoe. I had been taught how to make a fire using only one match, how to build a shelter out of my poncho, and to take four- and five-day canoe and hiking trips. These things seemed to have sunk in by osmosis; I hadn't liked all the tasks, but I had done the work.

When camp ended, Susan gave each counselor an evaluation. She was kind in her feedback to me, but I was not invited back.

When I returned to Princeton from Vermont, with three weeks to go before returning to Lake Forest, my mother took an interest in my suffering. My weight had shot up to 180 pounds. I was five feet six inches tall. I was wearing long sweaters and coats even in warm weather, thinking I could hide the weight. I was moping around the house, sleeping until all hours, and dreading returning to college. Out of frustration, and with no hope that I would ever learn any self-discipline, she took me to the family doctor at Princeton Medical Center.

"Sara needs some help or advice. She is obviously fat. I don't know how to help her."

The doctor weighed me. "You weigh 178 pounds. That's too much." What did he think I was? An imbecile? Of course, it was too much.

"We've tried to teach her some good eating habits but it seems useless," my mother added helpfully.

I looked at her with daggers in my eyes. This was not going well.

It was 1966. Tab was introduced in 1963, Diet Pepsi in 1965. For the first time, people could drink their breakfast thanks to Carnation's Instant Breakfast, introduced in 1964. Lower-calorie Cool Whip replaced whipped cream in 1965.[5] Big companies were jumping on the bandwagon to bring to the American public lower calorie foods. None of this helped me.

"I'm going to prescribe you a medicine that will keep you from getting so hungry," the doctor said. "And I want you to eat less at every meal."

He gave me a prescription for Preludin, a strong appetite suppressant, and directed me to take one pill each morning. Ten years later, Preludin would be banned from the market. It turned out to be speed, and very dangerous.

I loved Preludin! I started it the next morning, and within a week the weight seemed to be melting off me. I felt great, ready to take on the world. The drug was so effective at suppressing my appetite that I lost thirty pounds in a month. I returned to Lake Forest with a renewed spirit and a close-to-normal weight.

Preludin didn't just have an impact on my appetite; it seemed to make me smarter, too. I would sit down at my dorm desk to do homework, and I wouldn't get up until I had finished. This was unheard of for me. I was keeping focused, finishing my schoolwork, and getting to classes on time. I had lost all confidence in my ability to be a good student during my freshman year. Now, inexplicably to me, I was getting it back. My grades went up, my interest in studies went up, and my weight was going down. Once more, without any understanding or interest in understanding, I felt I had arrived. I felt as if I were part of the human race that attended and enjoyed college. I felt such satisfaction just being right where I was. A place where I belonged.

Preludin seemed to make me smarter with schoolwork, but it

5   The 1960s, Edward J. Rielly, p. 98

didn't make me any more intelligent socially. My phone rang one evening a couple of weeks into the academic year.

"Is this Sara?" a pleasant male voice on the other end asked.

"Would you like to go to the Fall Ball at the end of the month?" he asked once I assured him it was me.

Would I? Of course, I would. None of the kinds of kids I had hung out with during my freshman year, the slackers, would dream of going to a dance organized by the school. I wasn't going to hide in the darkness now that I was getting slimmer.

"Yes," I gushed. Someone had actually asked me on a date. We chatted about this and that and finally he asked, "Do you know who this is?"

I was so overwhelmed that someone had actually asked me out on a date, it had never occurred to me to ask who was doing the inviting. "I don't. Who are you? I'm so embarrassed."

"It's fine, but you should really ask next time." He didn't seem too fazed. He was a friend. More a friend of Dorothy's. Because she was spending the fall semester in France, he'd thought to ask me. "This will be a good story to tell Dorothy."

Like her, he seemed to brush off my lack of social graces. He might have told her, "That's Sara being Sara."

As the fall semester progressed, I got invited to more places and fun events. I was making new friends. But I was also starting a love affair with drugs. Not for one minute did I believe I was good enough to have these wonderful things happening to me. I was convinced it was all due to the Preludin. Being an addict, one pill a day soon wasn't enough. I thought taking two pills would be twice the fun. Then I started taking two or three in the evening to pull an all-nighter so I could finish a school project. I was so naïve about drugs and their consequences. I knew I shouldn't change the dosage on my own, but this was a doctor-prescribed medication. It didn't enter my mind that there were dangers or long-term consequences. I loved being awake late at night and early into the morning, when no one else was awake. Things seemed possible in the dark; I felt smarter and more adventurous. I developed a false sense of bravado, believing I could figure anything out, especially when it came to outsmarting teachers.

I would never have used the term "drug addict" to describe myself. These were just diet pills, and, anyway, I came from a good family. We had gone to a doctor and gotten his blessing. "These will help Sara lose weight," he'd said. He'd never mentioned any side effects.

Addicts came from bad families living on the edge. Everyone knew that. Growing up behind Ivy League walls, I had left for college with a naïve sense of what the world was like. My parents were academics. They valued learning/education and a career above all else. I was protected from what much of the world was like. My only knowledge of addiction of any kind came from the movies: Frank Sinatra in *Man with the Golden Arm*, for instance, which I'd watched on TV during vacation when the rest of the family was sleeping. That life of jazz and drugs felt so far removed from me that if anyone had used the word "addict" to describe my drug or sugar consumption, I would have thought they were nuts. But just like an addict, I had begun thinking I was special. I didn't have to do things the normal way. I could cut corners and end up in the same place as the "normies."

The more I thought I was getting away with something, the deeper was my conviction that I could fool anyone and do anything I wanted. I was stealing again, and getting good at it. Since my family wasn't around, I wasn't having rage attacks. I wasn't at war every day. I experimented with marijuana, which brought out laughter in me.

The first time I got stoned, I was walking back to my dorm room with a friend and I suddenly sang at the top of my lungs, "When the moon hits your eyes like a big pizza pie, that's *amore!*" As I belted out "amore," I abruptly realized I was standing in the middle of the quad, surrounded by four dormitories. It was the middle of the day. Anybody could have been watching or listening. A feeling of deep embarrassment wrapped itself around me.

I looked over at my friend, Mary. She had her hands on her knees to hold herself up, she was laughing so hard. Cautiously, I began laughing with her. I wouldn't go so far as to say I was laughing at myself, but as my embarrassment slipped away, the funnier the situation seemed. I liked being stoned.

Only six or seven months after taking my first dose of Preludin, I realized that my tolerance level was growing—that I needed more to accomplish the same thing: continuing to have no cravings for sugar, and maintaining my focus on my studies. I became miserable, grouchy, and completely annoying to myself and others as the effects of the drug wore off.

The worst part was, it wasn't suppressing my appetite anymore. I hadn't been cured of whatever made me eat after all. I couldn't understand why, smart as I was, I couldn't outsmart this monster thing inside of me. Rather than surrendering to the fact that I was out of control when I binged, I kept telling myself I just hadn't found the right answer yet. I kept deluding myself into believing I just had to try harder, that something was eluding me. But in the end, I couldn't do it. No food addict can.

My wonderful nights of staying up late, studying, writing class essays, and daydreaming turned into nightmares of impatience, anxiety attacks, and pain. One night, I ran out of cigarettes. I rushed to the basement of the dorm, where the cigarette machine lived, and put in my twenty-five cents. Nothing happened. I tried again. The damn machine was stealing my money. Within seconds, I became enraged. I was going to get my cigarettes, whatever I had to do.

I went searching through the large TV rooms where we played bridge, watched *Mission: Impossible*, and just hung out together. In one of the rooms, I found a heavy glass ashtray. I dashed back to the machine and heaved the ashtray at it. The thick glass shattered, exposing ten different brands of cigarettes. I pulled out huge pieces of the glass, left them lying on the floor, and filled my pockets with Tareytons, my cigarette du jour. *I won't be greedy*, I told myself. And I wasn't. I told everyone I saw for the next twelve hours that there were free cigarettes down in the basement.

In less than six months, I had gone from being an excited young woman who was losing weight and starting to have fun with her peers to someone who snarled at everyone, stretched too thin from fatigue and drug use. When I wanted something, I found more and more criminal ways to obtain whatever that thing was. Stealing, lying, smashing vending machines—it didn't matter to me, as long as the thing became mine.

Addicts are often seen by friends and family as having two sides to their personality: Jekyll and Hyde. Sara Jekyll was enthusiastic, curious, working toward health, and wanting friends. But Sara Hyde was nasty, rageful, lonely, and violent. A few adults had tried to tell me the consequences of letting Hyde have too much power—what it looked like and felt like from their perspective. But no one in my immediate circle knew that food addiction was even a disease, and in my opinion, I only had a weight problem. If I could just lose weight, everything would be okay. I rejected any other idea. I would listen periodically to the feedback and advice of kind people about my behavior, but I couldn't grasp the connection between my bingeing and the unmanageability of my actions. I would want to change in the moment, but the second Hyde took over, I had total amnesia. So I continued to live at the mercy of my addictions. My behavior never changed. In fact, it just kept getting progressively worse.

6

Europe

I was desperate to get away from college. There is an actual word in recovery language for what I wanted: a geographic, which means moving to a new place, hoping against hope that moving will solve all of one's problems.

When Dorothy returned from France, we were roommates once more. She described living in the city of Dijon, going to the university there, and taking wonderful day trips in the eastern part of France in such an appealing way that even though I hated studying French— had barely gotten a passing grade in it in all the years I'd taken it in school—I became determined to go. LFC sent twenty students each fall for a semester abroad. I signed up to study French language for the second half of my sophomore year, implored my parents to fork out the extra money, and was accepted into the Dijon program for the fall of 1967.

Dijon is two hours southeast of Paris within the Burgundy region. The center of the city would become a UNESCO World Heritage Site in 2015, but in 1967, it was a working-class town most famous for its mustard. The smell of Dijon mustard was everywhere, permeating the air day and night.

When I first arrived and walked the sidewalks, I kept thinking, *Something is different here.* By the third day, I'd figured it out. There were older people, people in their seventies and eighties, walking slowly and unsteadily, making their way up the sidewalks. Not only had I never seen this many people out walking as means of transportation, I'd never seen so many elderly people in one place. It occurred to me that the US hid its elderly in rest homes or other places—that they were not encouraged to be out in public. I didn't know if that was actually true, but I knew that what I was witnessing was not American.

Once we all arrived, we were each placed with a French family interested in America and Americans, who provided a room and breakfast for the duration of the three-month program. We were expected to join the family in their activities and practice our French.

I was the second student my family had hosted. The year before, a student from California had stayed with them. She'd been outgoing and had enjoyed spending time with them, and they'd loved her. I was the exact opposite. I knew this because they told me so when they tried to encourage me to spend more time with them.

The family was socialist, one of many political parties in France, and loved discussing politics. Besides the two parents, there were three young boys—ten, eight, and six years old—all very active and in the same primary school together. They lived within walking distance from the university where I had my classes. Best of all for me, they lived five minutes away from my closest friend in the program, Melinda. Each evening, instead of spending time with my hosts, she and I walked home together discussing our day. I arrived long after dark and went straight to my room.

From Day One I was terrified of my family—terrified of speaking French, terrified of making a mistake. I avoided any interaction with them if possible. Each morning, I waited in my room, which was on the third floor of a very modest home. It looked a lot like my dorm room, with a twin bed and chest of drawers. My suitcase stood in a corner and became a table of sorts. The walls had a few framed pictures of different cities in France. I must have spent a lot of time in that room doing homework, but mostly I recall my daydreaming, which was becoming a serious problem. I'd begun to prefer living in my head. I was either plotting and directing the future or reliving the past, often changing it with each rerun. I was also eating a lot of sugar and grains. Looking back, I'd more or less entered an altered state of being. For lack of a better word, I might call that state a "brownout." I was neither passed out nor present for my life. It seemed too painful. I was fat and full of fear. Life was more pleasing in my head, and also, in some strange way, I was protecting my sanity by staying checked out.

Lying in my bed in my room, I would listen to the clattering of dishes and the chattering of happy voices downstairs while the family had breakfast, got ready for school and work, and then left together. Only then would I go down to the large farm table in the kitchen where they had left me a French breakfast: baguette and butter, coffee, warm milk, and a bowl for my café au lait. When I was done eating, I gathered everything I needed for the day, left the house, and met up with Melinda or my other friend, Cassie.

Cassie and I had left the United States in late August, two weeks before our semester began. Together, we'd flown Icelandic Airlines, the student airline, to Luxembourg for one hundred dollars. It had been the cheapest flight available—and the most fun. We were twenty years old, and this was the first time for both of us being in Europe without our parents. We were excited and much awed by the prospect of our "big adventure." From Luxembourg, we had planned a trip that would take us to Brussels, Amsterdam, down to Paris, and then southeast to Dijon.

In Amsterdam, we stayed at a youth hostel in the red-light district, walking distance from the train station. Everything about Amsterdam was eye-opening to us. We'd see prostitutes sitting in their windows with the red light on, or we'd see the curtains drawn and the light turned off. I found it hard not to stare. I felt like Alice in Wonderland, in a world so foreign to me, completely unable to tear my eyes away from what seemed to me to be hidden away in the US.

We toured the Heineken beer factory, which gave out as much free beer as we could drink at the end of each tour. Drunk American students unused to drinking legally found it extremely funny to jump afterward into the putrid Amstel River. It only confirmed to the Dutch that Americans were a loud, obnoxious breed of people. We visited Anne Frank's hiding place, the spot where she and her family had lived for two years during World War II. It had been ten years since I'd seen the movie based on Anne's diary, and since my father had given me my very own diary. I'd eventually read the book and found Anne's ability to articulate her thoughts in her diary mesmerizing. She seemed to have profound insight for a girl of fourteen.

I wanted to have a place to put my thoughts, but I'd only ever written some twenty pages, and only when I was so miserable I didn't know what else to do. I called my diary Minna and wanted to write to Minna as if to a friend. But unlike Anne, whose generosity of spirit leapt from the page, I succeeded only in producing writing full of anger, self-pity, and resentment. The fact that Anne had existed, then died, and left a record of her life, fourteen years old and in hiding, had a profound impact on me.

At the hostel, I fell for a boy named Joe. Each evening, people would hang out talking, playing cards, getting to know each other. Joe was Dutch and was there every night. I wasn't sure if he worked there or just liked to hang out with the international students. He paid attention to me, so it had to be true love, I told myself. We talked, we went on walks, and after five days, when Cassie and I left for Paris, I promised to write and come back to visit. He never answered any letter I sent, nor was he at the hostel when I made it back at the end of October. I'm not even sure Joe was his real name.

Whoever he was, he took up a lot of space in my head for the next six weeks. I daydreamed about him the way I was daydreaming about most things. No matter what I did, I pretended he was watching, and I performed through my days rather than living them as a result.

In Dijon, I treated my host family as if they were hoteliers. After avoiding them in the mornings, I wouldn't come home at night until they were all in bed. I wrote in my journal how I longed to see Joe and never thought to mention the people I was staying with, who were putting me up and surely wanted to get to know me. I ate their food, slept under their roof, and refused any contact with them. They made attempts to have me join them in their activities. The mom suggested I watch the news with them, as the newscasters spoke clear, Parisian French that would help me improve my listening skills. Once, they invited me along to visit the boys' school. I went, nodding and smiling as I was introduced to teachers, praying no one would ask me any questions. They all fussed over me, but I was a terrible ambassador.

At the end of the semester, my family told the director I was too "*timide*," meaning shy. Both he and I knew I was anything but. I was scared to the point of paralysis, though, and didn't know how to push myself through, or even that I could.

My father would have said, "Sara, you can't see beyond your own nose. There you are in a brand-new place, living the life most Americans can only dream of, and you are stuck in your head, focusing only on what is wrong in your life."

He would have added and emphasized, "Grow up," but by that point in the conversation I would already have been out the door.

In early October, our director told us at a group meal that he had arranged an excursion to harvest grapes at a nearby vineyard. Burgundy is one of the most famous winemaking areas in France, and its wines were and still are some of the most sought after in the world. It was to be a two-day excursion, but if we ended up enjoying our time there, we had the option of staying a whole week.

The youthful owner of this vineyard was experimenting with hiring students—unskilled workers. The director wondered who among us wanted to go. Half of our group said yes, me included. Being away from classes and not having to confront my daily fears surrounding my host family was irresistible. I was being given a "get out of jail free" card. Yet I also said yes because a small kernel of curiosity had touched me somewhere deep down; I wanted to know more about these French customs, the kinds of things I'd never learn about in the United States.

My father would have been happy that my curiosity was not completely dead.

Both skilled and unskilled workers were to sleep near each other in dormitory-like lodgings, but we would have little contact with the skilled workers, known as *vendeurs* and *vendeuses*—harvesters who made their living traveling from vineyard to vineyard, cutting grapes and getting everything ready for the next step in making wine. The skilled workers were permanently bent over and aged from the hard work of cutting the grapes off thousands of vines before the autumn rains. Meanwhile, for us students, this was a holiday from school. Like the migrant workers in California, these lower-class farm workers of France had little choice in how they made a living. They were uneducated and poor, and their children started working at an early age. They looked with disdain, and maybe a little fear, at us students, who considered the whole thing a fun lark. If we turned out to be any good, would they lose their jobs?

My first day there, I met a young Dutchman two years older than me. I conveniently forgot about Joe for the moment and "fell" for this guy, since he was there and paying attention to me. Edward had come down from Amsterdam with his best friend. They were both in university there. Just like us, they were taking advantage of this opportunity to see what it was like to live and work in a vineyard.

Our group and the rest of the student hires lived together— sleeping in bunk beds, waking up at 5:30 a.m. to have coffee and start the day out at the vines. Breakfast would come after ninety minutes of work. We'd eat our baguettes and drink our cafés au lait at picnic tables beside the van that transported us from dormitory to vineyard. We'd stop work for two breaks and a one-hour lunch. Dark chocolate bars were served at every meal and break. After an early dinner back at the dormitory, we would party together as a group.

I thought of myself as fat at this point. I'd been gaining even more weight since arriving in Dijon. My hair had grown so long, it prac- tically reached my waist. It was thick and I often wore it in a braid. My hair was not the long, silky, dark hair flying gracefully with a shake of one's head that you saw in shampoo ads; mine was thick, wavy, coarse, Russian peasant hair. It was often dirty as well, as I didn't wash it often enough. It was just too much trouble, too much hair, and I didn't care enough. Eddie commented on my hair, though, seeming to admire it. He thought it was wonderful, and I took that to mean he thought *I* was wonderful. "I've never seen hair like yours," he told me, "It's amazing. How long have you grown it?"

I swelled up with pride, as long hair meant everything to me. "As long as I can remember, at least since I've been in college."

"And do you sing songs from *Hair*?" He was teasing but it was affectionate, not mean. *Hair* had recently been very popular on Broadway. He smiled at me, and I melted. He had a smile that was so open, and he seemed so confident.

"I never thought Americans would do this kind of work." He nodded in the direction where the *vendeurs* were housed. "We've always been told you're a bit lazy." Again, he smiled that smile. He was teasing me, although I knew he was telling the truth.

"Well, I'm not a normal American," I said. If I'd known how to swagger, that is exactly what I would have done.

"Let's go eat dinner and you can tell me why you're here and why you want to pick grapes," he said.

And that started my week of constant companionship with Eddie from Amsterdam. He asked me about me, about my life. He wanted to know what I thought about, what my opinions were. I didn't disabuse him of his notions of Americans; instead, I confirmed them and then emphasized that I was different! I hadn't experienced a boy taking that kind of interest in me, wanting to know so much. I didn't care what his motive was. It felt genuine. And he was handsome, and not too tall at five foot nine, a couple of inches taller than me. He wore his Dutch-blond hair parted on one side and falling boyishly over his forehead. His face was happy and open. He seemed always to be smiling or laughing. He was funny, good company, and spoke excellent English.

Each evening, Eddie and I would pair off and just talk and talk.

"I hate Vietnam and what's going on there," I told him one night, even though I barely knew how bad things had gotten.

"Aren't you being a bit naïve? Do you know all that is going on?"

"No, and I don't have to. People are dying, and why should they be dying?"

"Good question," he said. He was asking his questions in a tone not so different than my father's, but I didn't take it as criticism. I took it as encouragement to learn more. He told me about French involvement in Vietnam and how the Americans had moved in. Since he wasn't American, he was giving me an observer's view.

"How come you speak such good English?" I asked him on the second night we were there.

"We have to learn it in school, along with French and German. No one can pronounce Dutch words. We couldn't communicate with anyone if we didn't learn your language." His fluency was impressive.

"Most Dutch people speak at least one other language in their jobs, too."

It was so easy being with him. He made me feel that I had opinions worth listening to, even if he didn't agree with them. Time could have stood still for all I cared. I wanted these minutes and days with Eddie to last and last.

The *Vendange*, or harvest, is hard work. The girls were given cutters. We would pull the grapes away from the vine with our left hand, then stick the cutter in and cut the grapes off with our right hand. We carried pails with us and the grapes went right into them. We cut our fingers. We weren't allowed to wear gloves because then it would be too hard to feel the stem that we were to cut. We were told that we wouldn't become a good *vendeuse* until we'd cut our fingers at least seven times.

When our pails were full, we'd signal one of the guys who walked the long aisles of grapes with a huge straw basket on his back, and in our grapes would go, making his load heavier and heavier. When his basket was full, he'd take it to a large vat and empty his contents. I was dying to walk in my bare feet over the grapes, but most vineyards had already switched to machinery for the task of crushing the grapes by then. I'd seen enough foreign-language films to have seen the men with their pants rolled up past their knees, squishing the grapes by slowly marching around and around in the huge vats. It hadn't occurred to me that it was hard work, probably much like walking in quick sand.

I loved the *Vendange*—this particular one, anyway. That second day, after I had met Eddie, I was so happy that I started singing.

Dijon was sunny and warm that fall. The multitude of greens that made up the grapevines and the azure blue of the sky created a scene like an exquisitely framed photograph. The clarity of the air and the natural sounds of a working vineyard took my breath away. Maroon grapes bursting out of their skins hid behind the sparkling vines. All of us students were in a fabulous mood. The smell of stomped grapes, along with the dark chocolate and cigarette smoke, was intoxicating. My friends from school were near me, and I was in love! There seemed no other way to let out the abundance of feeling I had inside, so I sang as loud as I could.

I could carry a tune; I wasn't embarrassing myself. I started with Beatles songs, and when the others joined in, I felt encouraged to sing every rock and roll song I knew. We moved on to Joan Baez, Bob Dylan, and popular folk songs. I became the singing *vendeuse*.

The skilled workers were not amused. I was breaking an unwritten protocol of vineyard ethics. Eddie thought I was terrific. He and my other friends cheered me on to sing more and more, their joining in and singing loudly with me kept me going.

We were given bread, chocolate, and wine with every meal and at every break—heaven for a food addict. But I didn't binge. I ate way too much, as I had no idea what a normal meal looked like, but I wasn't bingeing. I knew the difference in my gut. Bingeing meant I had lost control of what and when I ate and I, under my own power, could not stop myself, whereas eating too much at meals was just that. I hadn't yet lost control; I just didn't know what a normal portion was because I had either undereaten or overeaten for so many years.

The hole in my soul was full. I felt attractive to someone. I felt love instead of longing, and a phenomenal sense of happiness and contentment.

Eddie told me from the very beginning that he had a girlfriend back in Amsterdam, but I didn't pay much attention. He certainly wasn't warning me off. It was just another piece of information about him, and I was living one day at a time. Every part of me that hated to feel vulnerable refused to think realistically about the future. Besides,

Eddie was Dutch and they seemed to think differently about relationships. I thought maybe it didn't matter that there was a girlfriend
in the mix, and I daydreamed about being with him. My experience
told me that my dreams wouldn't come true—I was never a boy's first
choice—so it was easier to stick my head in the sand, and fill it with
my many rationalizations, and choose not to think about anything
unpleasant. The idea that I could just have fun and get to know this
person never occurred to me—never. I was so desperate to find love,
to be loved, that with every boy I met, I started building a white picket
fence in my dreams, with wedding bells ringing in the background.

Eddie and I would end up staying in touch over the years. Over the
years, he would ask me why I'd never told him that I loved him. How
could I have told him? I already knew I'd be rejected, and I would
never let myself be that vulnerable. I was afraid. I would have denied
it at the time, but fear was underneath everything. I was afraid of my
parents, of their disappointment in me, of doing anything that was
my own idea. I was so afraid of them that I was enraged at them all
the time. I was afraid of vulnerability, of any kind of intimacy. I was
afraid that how I thought about myself was actually the truth, and
people would laugh at me if they saw my insides. And my fear told me
that if I put trust in anyone, they would abandon me. I was driven by
my fears. What expectations I put on people like Eddie. I was too terrified to admit to deep feelings; yet, I longed to be paired up in a permanent relationship. Which meant that Eddie had to do all the work,
without any indication from me whether to keep going forward or
not. Only many years later did a therapist ask me, "You thought he
had ESP, he could read your mind? Isn't that a heavy expectation to
put on anyone?"

When I was little I had horrible nightmares of killing my sister by
accident, of being eaten alive. I would wake up and not be able to go
back to sleep. Then I'd numb my fears with sugar and carbohydrates.
It worked enough of the time that it became a habit.

Maybe, if anyone had known that I used food to medicate my fears so early on and done something to correct that behavior, I might not have eventually crossed the line into addiction. But that's not what happened.

At the end of that week I returned to Dijon, and I was there for about two weeks when I got on a train to Amsterdam to see Eddie's family for my mid-term break.

Eddie met me at Central Station. It was a musty place, full of people coming and going, and I watched the large letters and numbers on the screens clickity-clacking new arrival and departure times. I'd written to him to ask if I could come and he'd wrote back an enthusiastic yes. I'd floated through the intervening two weeks.

"Welcome to Amsterdam," he greeted me with a big grin. "Where everything is possible."

Did he mean the city or us?

He picked up my bag and guided me toward the carpark with his arm on the small of my back. How different this was from two months earlier, when I'd headed to the red light district with Cassie. My heart soared.

"My mother is so excited to meet you. You're her first American," he told me. "Mine too." He winked at me—not the wink of a lecherous man but of an open-faced, smiling schoolboy.

I worried that I was blushing, so I just lowered my head.

"Sasha has lots of plans for you while I'm at my classes."

My heart sank. There really was a girlfriend. We were driving in his tiny NSU Prinz car from Amsterdam to one of the wealthier suburbs of Amsterdam. The land was absolutely flat, just like the Dutch paintings I loved—three-quarters sky and one-quarter land.

We were following a tributary of the Amstel River. "It freezes over during the winter and people will skate to work!" Eddie said proudly. "Everyone here loves to skate."

He chattered about his home while I stayed silent. Inside, I was so happy to see him, and encouraged that he was excited to have me there. But there was Sasha.

Now that I was in Amsterdam, he explained their relationship. "We've gone out since she was twelve and I was fifteen," he told me matter-of-factly. "Neither of us has ever gone out with other people. We're like better than friends."

I tried to interpret what that meant. Was he telling me he was open to a new relationship?

I met Sasha later that evening. She walked over from her family's home a few streets away. She was in her last year of what Americans call high school. She couldn't stay long—she had homework to do—but she stayed long enough for me to realize she was a real, live human being. I didn't want to like her. I wanted her to have warts on her face or to behave really badly. In fact, she was a very lovely-looking girl, about the same height as Eddie, with the requisite Dutch blond hair that fell to her shoulders. She had a handsome face with a strong Roman nose that gave her an air of confidence and strength. She was friendly toward me and invited me to come to her class the following day.

Starting that fall and for the many years I knew both of them, I spent time with Sasha but I never really got to know her at all. We never really connected. She was probably as wary of me as I was of her, and I was usually looking for her faults: she didn't seem warm-hearted enough, her English wasn't as good as Eddie's. But we developed a kind of dance of cordiality, based on both of us caring for Eddie.

Eddie lived with his mother. His father had died a number of years earlier and left the family comfortable financially, with a three-story townhouse. Eddie showed me up to the guest room on the top floor. Sasha had left by then, so I joined him and his mother for dinner, a simple meal of sausage, potatoes, and a cooked vegetable. His mom, who spoke no English but was very kind to me, soon excused herself and went to bed.

Eddie and I stayed awake for hours, drinking beer and talking. What would stay with me was the ease of being with him. My opinions seemed intelligent. There were never awkward pauses when I couldn't think of something to say, except when the subject of Sasha came up.

That night after dinner, I brought her up again, articulating my concern over her, albeit in an immature way: "Is Sasha going to be mad that I'm here?" I was future tripping about being in a relationship with Eddie but could only ask teenage questions.

"You're taking everything too seriously," he told me. "Sasha doesn't mind. That's the way we are here in Holland." He took my hand and kissed it. "Really, stop worrying. There's nothing to worry about."

I wanted to believe him, but it was hard to understand his intentions. I think he genuinely liked me, but he clearly wasn't in the same mental space as I was. I wanted to be a person who could stop worrying, someone who would stop thinking what everyone in the world was thinking about me. I wanted to be more like Eddie, but that was impossible because of my intense personality—and because of my food addiction.

Each day for the next three days was the same. In the morning, Eddie went to his university classes. I either spent time alone, reading or writing, or hanging out with Sasha. I wasn't able to relax around her, so I counted down the hours until Eddie came home around 5:00. When he did, he, his mother, and I would have a typical Dutch dinner of cold cuts or sausage with potatoes and vegetables. Then I would come alive. He and I would stay awake late, talking and drinking beer, and during those chats I felt relaxed—as relaxed as I'd ever felt, at least. I didn't have to be anywhere, I didn't have to be anyone. I didn't have to work at being me. I could just sit down, let go of my anxieties, and wish the evening would last forever, enabling me to enjoy my beer and my friend and the evening ahead of us.

The last night I was there, Eddie's mother cooked a *Rystafel* dish in my honor and Sasha and her parents were invited over to join us. *Rystafel* means "rice table." It's an elaborate meal served with as many as thirty side dishes, originally cooked to impress foreign visitors with the exotic abundance of Dutch cuisine. In fact, Dutch cooking was generally not very imaginative, but the *Rystafel* was the exception.

The meal must have taken hours to prepare. Eddie's mother, shy and sweet, never said a word to me, yet she treated me like royalty. With a little urging from Eddie, she insisted that I return in December before I went back to the United States. Of course I said yes.

Then the visit was over, and it was time to go to the train station. I met three friends from Dijon at the station. They remembered Eddie from the *Vendange* and were pleased to see him. But now we were no longer alone. I felt cheated because I wanted a romantic good-bye. Instead, he hugged us all, waved good-bye, and left for his classes. Just like that, the sun went behind a big grey cloud. I no longer stood in his warmth. I was just fat Sara, on my way to Copenhagen with my three friends.

I got crazy in the train, too loud, too quick to tell stupid jokes, acting just like the "ugly Americans" I abhorred. I no longer felt at ease in my skin but like an actress pretending everything was fine, thank you very much. All I wanted was to curl up in the fetal position and cry for the entire train ride. But I wasn't about to let my friends see the hurt and confusion I felt. Better to box it all up inside, eat whatever was in front of me, and act out.

The rest of that semester is mostly blurry. I continued to treat my host family's home like a hotel. I followed Melinda everywhere. Like Tami at summer camp, Melinda was outgoing, well liked, and had no fear of speaking French or making mistakes. She had a gorgeous figure, too, which I later learned she maintained by bingeing and throwing up. Neither one of us knew what the other did with food in private. She could see I was gaining weight, but I had no idea that she was as obsessed as I was with food and her weight.

French events were planned for us. We took a cooking class and made escargots and coq au vin. When the cook showed us how much wine to pour into the coq au vin, he said "*juste un tout petit peu*" (just a very little), and poured in two bottles of white wine with a huge grin on his face. We thought that was hilarious and got very drunk as we ate our meal and drank more bottles of wine.

On the third Sunday in November, the local vineyards opened up their cellar for wine tasting. All the grapes had been crushed, relieved of their skins, turned into juice, bottled, and set aside in cold cellars to ferment. The wine we'd help make would be offered at a wine tasting in three to four years. This November Sunday, we were sampling from three-year-old, and older, harvests.

At every vineyard, the tasting room floors were covered with sawdust. Each one of us brought a "*tasse à vin*"—a specially designed tasting cup—into which a very small amount of each type of wine was poured. The expert rolled the wine around in his *tasse à vin* to see how much sediment fell to the sides. Taking a small sip, he swished it around in his mouth to differentiate the myriad flavors in the wine. Then he spat it out onto the sawdust.

That's what the expert did. We students from LFC hoped that our *tasse à vin* would be filled to the top. We swallowed each sip, having no idea how to articulate the nuanced flavors. All that mattered to us was getting drunk.

Goal achieved: I threw up all over the backseat of the car of the sweet French man who'd offered to drive me back to Dijon.

The semester in Dijon ended. My mind had already traveled back to Amsterdam. I was going to spend two nights in Eddie's guest room in the Amsterdam suburb, purportedly visiting both him and his mom. I packed up my belongings and said good-bye to my college friends, knowing I'd see them all in Lake Forest at the end of January.

No grades had come out yet but before I left I did meet with the director, who conveyed my host family's disappointment in me. Once again, the feedback was kind—that I was *"timide."* They could have added "lazy," "made no effort," "fat," and any number of other traits that were true. Instead, they'd left it at "shy."

What no one said and perhaps no one had the words for was that my eyeballs only looked inward. I thought about myself 100 percent of the time, seven days a week. I wasn't a mean person, but the disease of addiction, characterized by self-absorption and self-centeredness, did not allow for the ability to feel genuine compassion unless it somehow served my needs. So I was stuck in a place of extreme fear of losing something I had or not getting something I wanted. I rushed off to Amsterdam without a word of gratitude to this French family that had put up with me in their home for three months. I rushed off to where I thought the something I wanted resided.

When I arrived, Eddie was waiting for me at the train station. "You're here," he said, as if he had been waiting for this moment also. He grabbed my bag and my arm with excitement. The mischievous look in his eyes was there. "We're going to have fun."

He may have said that out loud, maybe not. His eyes said it all, though. He was such a schoolboy with his blond hair falling over his forehead and his big, open smile, which greeted not just me, but life. He had such a confidence about him, such a sense of certainty, and those were the qualities that made him seem much more a man to me.

He whisked me to the car and deposited everything in the trunk. Then we walked, hand in hand, to a café for some food and a beer. We fell right into talking as if no time had passed.

"I'm on school holiday now, so all my time is yours," he said.

Did he mean that, or was Sasha coming along with us?

As if reading my mind, he added, "Sasha and her family are really busy at the moment so you won't see much of her."

Two nights and three days flew by. It was Christmastime, and Amsterdam was dressed up in her best electric colors. The sun would set at 4:30 p.m., and all the city would light up, augmenting my magical feeling of being in love. If I expressed doubt or looked forlorn, Eddie would take me by my shoulders and say, "Don't be silly. You worry way too much. Let's have fun."

I was completely seduced by his nearness, his touch, his words. I tried to resist him, thinking it was "the right thing to do," but my resolve melted in the face of his endearing words each time. I didn't yet have a language for or understanding of how much fear and terror I lived in, and that what I thought of as "right" or "wrong" was actually a way of trying to protect myself from being vulnerable, from getting hurt. I didn't have any idea if I had a sense of integrity at my core. Eddie could pull me into his sphere just by smiling and telling me not to be so silly.

Everything I knew about falling in love came from books and movies and my own fantastical imagination. No one had told me that falling in love leaves one wide open, unzipped, and that you have to breathe deeply to even attempt some sort of balance. Addicts like me don't like "unzipped," "exposed," and "uncertainty." Food—in the form of sugar, grains and carbs—was what fed that hole, so, desperate as I was to feel grounded, that state of being was elusive.

I had to find some logic to rationalize the way I built up walls, so I made moral judgments, based on some internal rulebook of what was right and what was wrong. Not having any perspective to question where those rules came from, I never really thought about that "rule book." I never asked myself if it was mine or if it came from a parent.

As an adult, I have questioned those rules. My mother was a perfectionist and her rules were very black and white. In her eyes, I was bad. I almost always made bad choices. If someone was upset, the fault must be mine. I can't remember one instance in my life when she gave me the benefit of the doubt. "Don't upset other people," she always said. And if I did? She certainly never said, "You'll burn in hell," but my fear of her anger, disappointment, and final verdict on my behavior was hell on earth.

Once I got into recovery for my food addiction, I started to recognize the many forms my fears took and how they held me hostage. I began to see those "rules" for what they were: a child's interpretation of the many do's and don'ts that were said to me by the adults in my world. I saw that I accepted as a given that one never upset others. That one should go out of their way to make sure others were happy. Somehow I had the muscle to lie, steal, and cheat, but the fear of upsetting others and of their not liking me was crippling.

So I would tell myself that the right thing to do was leave Eddie alone—that he belonged to someone else. Then we'd be together talking, having fun, being relaxed, and my rules would go out the window. I didn't care. It was just like bingeing. I'd make a promise to myself, break it, and then hate myself and binge more. The absolute only way I felt any sense of peace was to be physically near Eddie. And this was all before there was any relationship other than a strong flirtatious friendship with Eddie.

On December 22, Eddie took me to the shuttle that would take me out to the airport.

"When will I see you again?" he asked, as if it was a given.

"I have to work something out with the college," I told him. "And I will, you bet I will."

He was holding my hand, looking intently at me, that slightly amused grin on his face—he clearly wasn't having any difficulty with his "two girls"—and then he hugged me, kissed me chastely on the mouth, and deposited me on the bus. As it pulled away, he stayed rooted to the same spot, waving good-bye.

So far, our "relationship" was not physical; rather, it was turning into a deep friendship. Were I more mature, I might have taken this as a sign of where Eddie stood.

I put all my belongings in the overhead bin, sat down, and proceeded to cry all the way to the airport. I didn't want to leave. This felt like my one chance at real happiness as I defined it: being loved by someone. What I could bring to the relationship did not enter into the equation. I was a fat nothing and Eddie could love me into a someone. I didn't want to go home and have to deal with my real existing relationships—the ones I had with my mother and father. With them, I knew, I was not only a nothing, I was a *disappointing* nothing. I didn't want to go back to college. The days in front of me seemed stretched out like a highway in the west, nothing but road as far as my eyes could see.

I cried as I took my belongings off the bus and entered the airport. Suddenly, I realized I'd forgotten my camera on the shuttle. On a dime, my emotions switched into panic mode. I rushed back, but the shuttle was gone. I paced and breathed heavily, checking my watch every thirty seconds, as I waited for the next one. I went back into Amsterdam. Time couldn't move fast enough. I could barely sit still. From the long nothingness, I had now moved into a state where Mexican jumping beans inhabited my entire body. I stood up, I sat down, I stood up again and walked the aisle.

Thirty minutes later, I was back at the shuttle stop. The driver had turned in my camera. I was flooded with waves of relief. My body was buzzing from the panic and anxiety. All my tears were gone as I once more headed to the airport, wondering if I'd make my plane in time.

On the plane, which I made in plenty of time, my body slowed down. I was exhausted, but instead of going to sleep I found myself back on the highway whose furthest point fell off the earth, and crying. Poor, poor me. I knew no in between.

For years, I swung from panic attacks to misery and despair. I fueled it all with sugar. Even if I'd known I was throwing gasoline on a fire, I couldn't have done differently. It was what I knew. It was a knee-jerk reaction to every emotion. I had to find sugar, preferably ice cream, all the time. I thought it was the solution. Yet, my emotional life was on a slow but steady downhill ride. My solution was slowly killing me.

Back at Lake Forest, I had one goal—getting back to Eddie and Amsterdam. I had to pick a major so that I could graduate. When I first arrived at LFC, I'd thought I'd major in English and write a great

American novel. Then I was put into an 8:00 a.m. class that I rarely showed up for, and I squeaked by with a D-. Then I thought psychology would be fun. I took Introduction to Psych and was completely bored and again squeaked by with a D-. The semester before I went to Dijon, I'd taken Intro to Art History, which I loved, and I'd actually gotten a B. This prompted me to declare my major as art history that January of 1968. I could sit in the dark, look at slides of masterpieces of painting and sculpture, and be transported back to Europe. All I had to do was keep myself awake during the morning classes.

Memorizing the art—what it was called, where it was housed, and what year it was created—seemed to come easily to me. I also discovered a skill that almost guaranteed I got good grades: helping my classmates whose ability to memorize wasn't as good as mine. I would sit with them and test them on their memorizing of slides. Since I was immune to suggestions on improving my life, I had to learn these skills by accident, and I found that tutoring others improved my own grades. I got a part-time job in the Art History Department as well.

I also started taking Preludin again. It had been a while since my debacle with the cigarette machine. I'd run out of the pills months before I was supposed to have finished the prescription, so it had been a long time, and the drug worked as it had when I first started using.

I isolated myself from the college community by getting off their food plan. Because I worked for the Art History Department, I could come and go in the department building as I pleased. Soon I began pulling all-nighters there—finishing the filing, high on speed, and then writing lengthy letters to friends, giving my opinions on everything in the world. I'd write to Eddie; to my friend Georgia in California; I even wrote to my cousin in Memphis who I had no relationship with but who, I thought, would love to hear what I thought of the world.

It was on one of these nights that I discovered that there was going to be a first-ever semester abroad program in Florence, Italy, the following year. Whatever I had to do to be included on that trip, I became determined to do it. I was getting good grades now that I was an art history major, and the professors liked me. I was around the department a lot and they saw me as a good worker. I was almost completely isolated from the rest of my student friends, living in my head where I was comfortable, and I had a dream that now seemed like it might come true. I applied and was accepted to the program in Florence.

The rest of the semester crawled by in a brown haze. It had to be a thick, very self-centered haze, since during that time Martin Luther King, Jr. and Bobby Kennedy were murdered. The world turned upside down with students flooding the streets in agony at the mess our elders had made. The war in Vietnam seemed never-ending, and my peers were furious.

My nights, meanwhile, were filled with heady words to friends on the state of our messed-up world. But during the day I was fully ensconced in where I would be the following year. My life felt like a soap opera. I acted out the appropriate disbelief and disgust at our country's politics, but it was nowhere near the top of my list of priorities. I had told Eddie I was coming back and we were planning to meet up in December, before I had to be in Florence.

My life had meaning. I had a goal. Thanks to the Preludin, I was taking off weight one more time. I lived for December, and I wasn't about to show up fat when Eddie picked me up at the train station.

In February 1969, I lay in bed sick. Curled up in my double bed in the Pensione New York in Florence, Italy, I felt beat up. My head was stuffed up, I ached all over, and I drifted from a drug-like sleep to hazy awakeness. I pulled my head under the pillows completely, unaware of the Arno River flowing by outside my window. So much for this room with a view. I could have been anywhere in the world, for all I saw or cared.

In my half-asleep mind, I was running a film of the months since I'd left the US. I had been in Hamburg, Germany; Amsterdam, Holland; and Naples, Capri, and then Rome in Italy. Now, all the gorging on places and experiences had caught up with me. And replaying scene after scene of Hamburg with Eddie, I told myself I was absolutely and completely finished with him and Sasha and the whole crazy triangle.

My life had come to a grinding halt. I couldn't even eat right now. Still, my weight, though hovering around 150 pounds, was coming back on. With the help of Preludin and other drugs, it was a slow gain. But it was a gain nonetheless.

In December, I had flown straight to Hamburg, where Eddie was now living and working. My days there were a nonexistent blur until he arrived back in his studio apartment at 5:30 p.m. Then we went out dancing at bars, drinking beer, and picking up our nonstop conversations as if a year hadn't passed. We made love the first night for the first time. I was shy and scared but happy to have finally committed physically.

After a week in Hamburg, Eddie insisted I return to Amsterdam with him for his Christmas break. There I was back in my third-floor guest room in his home, but this time Sasha slept in his bedroom with him. I was put in my place fast, and the hurt was awful. At night, I lay in bed working up resentments, feeling incredibly sorry for myself, and wondering why I couldn't figure out what was wrong with me. During the day, I covered it up with smiles, people pleasing, and lots of food. I couldn't wait to get away from him, from her, from feeling so stupid and taken advantage of. I couldn't eat enough or fast enough. For a year, I'd lived to return to Europe and to Eddie. He'd given me a week of pure joy, then turned around and slapped me in the face so hard that I'd crumbled into little pieces inside, hating myself for being weak and vulnerable—hating him for being so mean.

When I left, I swore to myself it was over. *Get on with your life, Sara.*

Florence, the city of the Medici, was the perfect antidote for me. I loved that city with a fierceness I didn't know I had in me. I walked the narrow streets, looking at the intriguing, beautifully built doors that hid entire households behind them. I wasn't sitting in dark college classrooms looking at slides of Florentine architecture; I was there, in the flesh, gazing on Brunelleschi's Duomo, Ghiberti's golden doors, and Giotto's paintings. Maybe every young student feels this way, but I was twenty-one years old and had lived in London, Geneva, Dijon, Berkeley, Princeton, and Philadelphia, and nowhere had filled me with such wonder, such awe at the beauty that humans could produce.

The three months that the LFC Study program was there were flying by far too fast. I'd hiked the hills around Assisi and gazed out over the countryside of St. Francis and thought, *This looks exactly like it did seven hundred years ago.* I'd sat at one of the canals in Venice watching the water taxis go by and thought, *People have lived here long before me. Life has happened, art has been created. I'm walking where Michelangelo and Leonardo walked.* I was aware of history; a fledgling awareness was breaking through my walls of self-absorption. For hours at a time, I wasn't the center of the universe. Eddie and Amsterdam were relegated to a small part of my consciousness.

I'd run into a friend from Princeton who lived in Florence. He had been to Lebanon and brought back hashish. Since then, high as I was on Florence, I'd also been high on my friend's drugs. I'd spent more time stoned with him than participating in events with my college group. When he asked me to take hashish back to Princeton to give to his cousin, I'd said, "Of course, why not." I wanted to be cool. Besides, he was also giving me a lot to take back to LFC to share with my friends.

From my sick bed, I contemplated not returning to the States, not graduating in two months. Would I actually throw four years of a college education out the window? I was sick and feverish and way too scared. I knew it wasn't a real question. I'd never not return. My parents would kill me.

After a week in bed, I emerged from my sick bed ready to embrace what was left of our time in Florence. I walked everywhere, taking visual snapshots in my mind of every nook and cranny. I packed my bags and my hashish and started plotting once again how to return to Europe—only this time to Florence. Then I set about getting in my own way.

I carried the drugs with me as two friends and I crossed into Yugoslavia (now Croatia) to drive down the Dalmatian Coast. I didn't tell them that I had put us all at huge risk of being thrown in jail in a Communist country. I was just being my regular, thoughtless self, thinking only about what would work for me. When I did tell them at the end of the trip, I couldn't understand why they were disturbed and shocked. (One woman never spoke to me again. The other, when a reunion dinner was proposed thirty years later, was very reluctant to see me.)

I crossed three more borders before returning to Luxembourg to fly to the US. I came through Customs with three bricks (about the size of a brick of clay, but flatter) of hash strapped around my waist. I thought I was hip, slick, and very cool. I thought how much people would admire me. I should have believed in a god at that point, that someone somewhere was looking out for me, doing for me what I was incapable of doing for myself. But no—I just told myself I was too cool, too hip, to be caught, even though I spent my hours on the plane completely terrified.

Two months later, I graduated college. It was June. The Summer of Love 1969 was just beginning. I held a college degree in my hand but was totally unprepared for the world. I didn't want to work. I certainly didn't want to go to graduate school, even for art history. I would have to learn German, and that was way too much trouble. I wanted to be the ultimate hippie, going to concerts (I made it to Woodstock), traveling, and just having fun. I felt no attachment to anything—not a career, not my family, not any person. I thought I was footloose and fancy-free.

I shot out of the academic cannon of undergraduate education in no particular direction with no skills except for bullshit. On one hand, I felt superior to my classmates who had to go to work or to the army; on the other, I still believed I was really a piece of shit who was completely unlovable. I was terrified of being found out. I knew only one way to deal with the whole frightening mess: eat, binge, and take lots of drugs.

7

Hippie Years in Europe

I talked my friend, Andi, into returning to Florence with me. Thanks to her father, a naval captain, we could book passage on an Italian freighter going from Norfolk, Virginia, to Brindisi, Italy—a cheap voyage reserved for naval families and friends. The catch was that there was no arrival or departure date, but once the boat did arrive in Norfolk, there was a quick turnaround. So we waited out the summer with no idea when we would be leaving, only that we had to be ready to get to Norfolk in as little as twenty-four hours if necessary.

I found a summer job at Buxton's Coffee Shop on Nassau Street in Princeton. I started bingeing almost immediately. The freezer in the kitchen was bursting with multiple flavors of ice cream, my "drug" of choice. My pay was so low that I rationalized the bingeing by telling myself that I had earned it. I was a complete pain in the ass. I was the newest waitress in this midsize and simply decorated coffee shop/ ice cream parlor—which, since it was summer vacation, was never crowded. I considered myself the smartest, most superior, and most efficient of everyone working there. I sped around on sugar highs, making sure everyone saw that I was not only doing my job but also theirs.

My arrogant attitude covered up the complete and utter despair that had returned with that first bite of ice cream. I couldn't believe

I had done it again. I couldn't put into words the desolation I was feeling. I was starting to believe that there was no answer for me, that I was jinxed and destined to live in hell for the rest of my life. *I'm leaving soon and then I'll figure it out*, I told myself with no awareness of having promised myself this exact same thing many times before. I didn't even try not to binge. I hated Princeton, hated being a waitress, hated everyone.

The pain became fear, the fear became panic attacks. If I wasn't curled up in bed with my head under the pillow, I was racing around trying to stay in front of the panic. *Why doesn't Andi call? I've got to get out of here.* I pleaded with the universe to make my next geographic just around the corner.

Andi called in late September to tell me that the ship was at port and we had to be ready to board three days later. I was packed, ready to go, and in Norfolk within forty-eight hours. On the train down, I prayed to some god I wasn't sure I believed in that I might please leave all the bingeing behind in Princeton. *Please God, I can't wait until we get to Florence—for the magic to start working. Please help me*, I implored.

The freighter that Andi and I were passengers on was transporting coal to Italy. From the captain's perch, it looked as if the coal storage took up half the boat. We were not allowed near there. Our stateroom was the size of a small bedroom. We had two bunk beds and I had the top bunk, where I spent the majority of my time reading and writing in my journal. One porthole window let in most of the light, and we had two small desks that sat side by side against one of the walls. The door had a lock, but it didn't seem very secure to me.

The captain, protective of us, his only passengers, had warned us about the men on the boat, that they didn't see women very often.

Though he didn't give specifics, he seemed to think we understood exactly what he was telling us. Sure enough, on three different nights, we watched the door knob wobble and shake as one of the crew attempted to get in. Each time, one of us jumped out of bed and stuck a chair under the handle. We weren't particularly scared—mostly because we were twenty-two. (You have to be twenty-two years old to put up with fifteen days at sea with nothing to do and a crew who hasn't seen women in a long time.) But we did keep the chair under the doorknob for the rest of the voyage.

We sat at the captain's table for meals and, as we were the only two passengers, we each sat on either side of him. The table was small and round and only his two other officers sat silently at the table with us. Neither Andi nor I spoke Italian and since the captain spoke English, all conversation was in English. He was a kind person. He called me Connie Francis because of my dark looks. Connie Francis was a ballad singer who'd crossed over from the Big Band days into early rock and roll. She had a beautiful voice—one I didn't appreciate because I considered myself a rock and roll baby. This reference dated the captain in my mind, and I was mortified because it wasn't cool to like Connie Francis. He did his best to amuse us during the long days by inviting us to come to the helm every day, even giving us the steering wheel for minutes at a time.

After fifteen long days at sea, we arrived a day late in Brindisi. We were scheduled to leave Rome that afternoon for Israel. We picked up our rental car and then my crazy, reckless, dangerous driving over one-lane roads crossing from the east of Italy to the west, fueled by sugar and anxiety, got us to the Rome airport with minutes to spare. Soon we were seated together on a flight full of noisy, joyful Sabras (Israelis born in Israel) going home.

Rome to Israel was about four hours' flying time. By the time we arrived at the airport halfway between Tel Aviv and Jerusalem, the passengers had quieted down. Andi and I had formulated an open-ended plan for our traveling that would take us first to my sister's kibbutz in Sde Boker, where she had been living for the past six weeks doing a semester abroad, then down to Eilat and finally up to Kfar Hess, where my cousin, Miriam, and her family lived. It had been two and a half years since the Six Day War. Emotions and fear still ran—and would continue to run—very high between Israelis and Palestinians. Andi, blond and WASPy-looking, was through passport control in a short time. I, on the other hand, apparently looked suspect to the airport police. I was fat, dressed shabbily, and likely had a look of fear on my face. I was detained and questioned. I was terrified.

The Israeli customs agents went through everything I'd brought with me. Since my normal arrogance wasn't at all helpful, I turned into a helpless victim. How could they possibly think that I, poor me, could be carrying weapons or bombs? I imagine that when they finally let me go, they did so thinking that only an entitled American girl could possibly be such a wimp.

When we were finally seated on the shuttle bus into Jerusalem, I burst into tears. This was not the start to our "big adventure" that I had been anticipating.

"Cheer up, Sara," Andi said. "We're on our way now. That's over and next stop is your sister's kibbutz."

"Oh great," I retorted. "She said we could come, but did she really mean it?"

I hadn't seen Vicki in nearly two years. In that time, she'd gone from a petite, cute-as-a-button junior in high school to a 240-pound woman. I hadn't seen her enough during my college years to take in her transformation. Now, I saw she was fatter than I was and, therefore, a worse person than I was. I didn't even know that I thought of fat people as bad, but I was sure I was a bad person with no control, and now I saw that she was a very bad person with even less control. That's how I operated and that's how I treated her.

She showed us around the kibbutz. "Your beds are here." She pointed to the humble dwelling where we'd spend our nights on this working Israeli farm. She picked oranges most of her days. "Unfortunately, I have a work shift so I won't see you at dinner."

"So we'll see you at breakfast?" I asked.

"No, I can't. I have another shift."

I frowned. "Are we going to see you at all?"

"I'm free for a little while tomorrow afternoon." She shrugged. "They work us students just as hard as if we lived here, so I don't really have any choice."

"Okay." Light was beginning to dawn in my dense head. "So, what are *we* supposed to do?" I asked, very irritated.

"I'll see you tomorrow," she said, and left, not bothering to answer my question.

I turned to Andi. "I can't believe it. We come all this way and she just treats us like shit. What's wrong with her? Why can't she be nice?"

"She is being nice, Sara," Andi said in her best peacemaking voice. "She is very busy. We don't have to stay. We can go to the Dead Sea and Be'er Sheva and be tourists in Israel."

Vicki was in complete avoidance mode with me. I refused to see it. I just thought she was inconsiderate and mean. We only stayed on the kibbutz for two nights. I don't even remember saying good-bye to her. We spent the next weeks traveling, and I put Vicki to the back of my mind.

Israel wasn't what I was expecting. It sits on the cusp of Europe and the Middle East. Culturally, it was bizarre and a bit dangerous for a naïve twenty-two-year-old girl. As long as Andi and I stayed close to tourist spots like the Dead Sea, we were fine. But when we drifted into the bazaar in Be'er Sheva, trying to buy goodies, we had to tangle with crafty Arab men who had a whole other way of negotiating the world, prices, interactions with women, and just being in their daily lives. Both of us felt uncomfortable, but I tried to hide it, pretending I wasn't the naïve girl from academic Princeton. To cope, I binged all day long on the honey pastries that were available everywhere.

We arrived at Miriam's home in mid-November. I spent a great deal of time trying to convince her what a good sister I was and how Vicki was so unreasonable.

"You need to give her space, Sara, and just leave her alone," Miriam said. "Things will work themselves out in the future."

"But I really need to talk about it. She was so mean to us."

"I don't want to hear it. I love both of you. I wouldn't listen to her badmouthing you either."

I just could not understand. I believed the world was exactly as I saw it. If someone else didn't see it that way, I felt it was my job to set them straight. I had a hard time letting go and respecting Miriam's wishes. I tried to sneak a few remarks in sideways, but Miriam wouldn't have any of it. She didn't even have to speak. All she did was give me a look like I was a child, which clearly said, "Stop."

By late November, as the Israeli part of our trip ended, Andi and I had been together twenty-four hours a day, seven days a week, for almost seven weeks. Though Andi was a year older than me, I was the louder, more forceful person. She wasn't shy in any way, and was game for pretty much anything, but I was still louder and bossier, so she often deferred to me. She had strong opinions, though, and when she expressed them, she didn't always agree with me.

Andi had let me plan our itinerary. She'd gone to Israel because I wanted to, she'd listened to me bitch about my sister and acquiesced 80 percent of the time to my preferences. But when she started to assert herself in small ways, I found her to be totally irritating. After seven weeks together, I found all number of infractions that annoyed me: she was too slow getting dressed in the morning; she didn't dress enough like a hippie; she wasn't putting up with me as much as she had in the beginning.

In time, I became full-on resentful. I was pissed all the time. I didn't like anything Andi did. I daydreamed of having a boyfriend and traveling with him instead of her. By the time our travels landed us on the island of Crete in early December, we were barely talking to each other.

In discomfort, we visited the palace of King Midas in the town of Heraklion. Then we hitchhiked to the eastern tip of Crete in a taxi driven so fast over the narrow cliff road that we feared for our lives. Completely oblivious, the Greek driver laughingly practiced his English with us. I bloated myself with cheap sesame biscuit cookies, consuming huge packages of them and stuffing down my resentful misery with each bite.

In the lovely village of Agios Nikolaos, walking on a spectacular beach one morning near the hostel where we were staying, I said to Andi, "We have to talk."

That was all the opening she needed.

"I like you so much, Sara, but you are so difficult to be with," she blurted out. "You've hurt me over and over, and I don't think you even know it. You act like you don't like me. You don't like anything I suggest. I've tried to support you with your sister, with your food, in the only way I know how—and it's not good enough for you. And most of all, I just hate it when you totally ignore me."

Like Mrs. X and my Dijon family before her, Andi was speaking kindly. I hid my head so she couldn't see my tears. I hated to cry. It made me feel weak. But as I listened to Andi, I knew she spoke the truth. Living with my anger all the time had made me so lonely.

We sat on the smooth white sand, looking out at a turquoise blue Aegean Sea, re-meeting each other. It felt unreal to me. It seemed like a stage setting, and we were the drama. Leaning against rocks in this beautiful place, we attempted to heal a broken relationship—broken because of me. I knew this now. I just didn't know what I could change or do about it. I didn't want to push Andi away. For the millionth time, I found myself praying for answers: *What is wrong with me? Why do I upset people so much?*

Andi waited while I cried. She hadn't wanted to hurt me, but she was relieved to finally spill out all her feelings.

"I'm so sorry, Andi," I finally said. "I don't know what happens to me. I just get so angry and then I think that everything you do is wrong. I feel possessed."

"We've been traveling together for a month and a half," she said carefully. "What if we took a break and found other people to go to Florence with?"

This wasn't an out-of-bounds suggestion. People of all ages were hitching or traveling all over Europe and farther into the east. There were plenty of opportunities to do this ourselves without feeling that we were being unsafe.

Still feeling a bit shaky, I agreed. "Okay, that's probably good. We could set a date to arrive in Florence and we'd both be there?"

"Yes, exactly. We could start by looking at the boards at the youth hostel tonight and also going to the American Express in Athens. I know we'd find rides easily."

Why didn't I let Andi take over more often? Clearly she had good ideas, and she voiced them in a way that felt so caring to me. Why did I reject everything she suggested? Was it a matter of not being able to trust anyone?

We walked slowly back to the youth hostel. I contemplated the fact that nothing about this spot had changed in thousands of years. Our little squabble was small in comparison to wars that had been fought here by Greeks, by Romans, by the French. Somehow I needed to grasp all that to my insides in order to say good-bye to this quiet, soothing beach. That I wasn't the only one who had fallen apart surrounded by such a beauty.

That night, I found a group of Americans traveling to Italy in a VW van. We all took the boat back to Athens the next day and then made a beeline to the American Express office. In those days, the American Express was travel central. Travelers like us went there for everything: to pick up mail, get money, make phone calls back to the United States, and meet other travelers. If any of us met someone we liked and wanted to see them again in another country, we would agree to meet up in the American Express office in whatever city or town.

Andi found another group of Americans she connected with—and so all was set. We'd meet at our pensione in Florence on December 21. My feelings of embarrassment and shame had passed. I was on a new adventure with new people, and once again I was singing that familiar refrain: *This time it will be different.*

But things were not different, and I spent much of the two weeks without Andi bingeing in secret, when and where I could.

Andi and I arrived in Florence within an hour of each other. Andi's traveling companions were still there, waiting with her, when I walked in. We weren't at the pensione more than thirty minutes before I was guiding everyone to the gelato place I had frequented so often the year before. At the gelateria, no sooner did that first taste of ice cream hit my taste buds and blood stream than I was craving more. I was genuinely happy to see Andi, but it would be years before I'd understand her confusion at seeing my pleasure about being together again while at the same time seeing how I was trying to get rid of her. I just wanted to get back to the gelateria and buy as much ice cream as I could consume without her noticing.

Andi's parents knew an American woman married to a Florentine man, and they invited us to Christmas Eve dinner. I had brought nothing with me from home but jeans—worn bare from my thighs rubbing together and full of holes covered by patchwork pieces of fabric—and old sweaters, all of which were dirty.

I'd bought an Arab dress at a market in Jerusalem that I was in love with. I'd wandered the streets of Old Jerusalem for hours looking for the perfect dress. I loved the embroidery all over the bodice and the bottom near the hem. The one I finally decided on was black, which set off the intricate hand embroidery. But it was true hippie-wear, and this family sounded quite conventional.

If Andi went without me, I'd feel jealous, lonely, and miserable. At the same time, I knew that if I went with her, I'd risk being a laughingstock because I didn't know how to dress. If I borrowed clothes from her, I'd be bursting out of them.

My way of coping was to slip back into feeling so sorry for myself, being the victim. *If only I'd done that . . . If only . . . If only.* From there, it was a downhill trip to, *What is wrong with me that I can't diet, that*

I can't stop eating? Why is everyone else so pretty and thin and I'm so ugly and fat? By the time we got to Christmas Eve dinner, I'd worked myself up into such a painful place that I was fertile ground to rationalize bingeing.

On January 2, knowing we needed to find jobs if we were to stay in Florence, we made our way to a Community Center bulletin board. Every scrap of paper was a notice looking for an au pair. I made a face at Andi. "We aren't going to have to be au pairs, are we? That's what everyone does."

She shrugged. "How bad can it be? And you'll get to practice your Italian!"

I frowned. "But I didn't come here to be someone's babysitter."

Not having given any real thought to work, I hadn't realized I'd need work papers to work in Italy. And what did I think I was qualified to do?

"Come on, Sara, stop your bitching. Let's just call and see what happens."

We each wrote down a phone number and went looking for a pay phone. Both of our calls were answered by Italian men, Antonio and Matteo, who turned out to be friends. They had figured out how to get a commission by brokering between families and potential au pairs. After we met them for coffee, we decided they were really just looking for available girls. But they did arrange interviews for both of us.

My family lived on the south side of the Arno river, not too far from the Ponte Vecchio. Behind an elaborate door was a huge villa that the wife had inherited from her family. On my interview day, I walked into a dining room/living room with a black-and-white checkerboard marble floor and a ceiling that had to be at least twenty-four feet high. The décor was spare, as one often finds in those old villas.

The wife, who spoke English, hired me after just a short conversation. I would be given room and board in exchange for taking care of five-year-old Jacopo. She showed me to a small cottage behind the main house with a twin bed, a wood stove, and a desk with a chair. I would be responsible for buying coal to warm the small room. I felt that it was too much trouble to organize buying coal. I would spend that winter being very cold.

Memory is a funny thing. I lived there for three and a half months, but I couldn't tell you what the kitchen looked like or what I did with my time. I read Jack Kerouac books and shivered in my little bed, dreaming about being a famous writer. I took Jacopo on walks to the Boboli Gardens and bought lots of crappy food that I ate in my room. Matteo and Antonio took Andi and me on day trips outside of Florence. Antonio and Andi fell in love, and Antonio asked her to marry him. For a short time, she contemplated staying in Florence and doing just that.

I was jealous of what I called Andi's good luck. Matteo seemed okay to me—a bit coarse, but I liked doing things as a foursome with him and the other two. I slept with him; that's what we did back then if you were dating. But I didn't consider him a boyfriend.

On one of our excursions, Andi and Antonio pulled me away from Matteo to talk to me.

"We don't want to hurt you," Andi said, "but you have to know that Matteo is talking about you behind your back."

I wasn't sure I wanted to know more. "What do you mean?"

"I was with him at a gathering," Antonio said, "and he told people that he was sleeping with a fat pig."

In a photograph of me sitting on Matteo's lap that would survive decades, he is slender, somewhat good looking, dark, and dressed casually. I am very heavy by comparison. I have a bandana wrapped around my long brown hair, which is braided and falling over my right shoulder. I'm smiling but I don't look happy. I'm twice his size.

Even though I wasn't crazy about Matteo, I had fooled myself into thinking that he might really like me. When Andi and Antonio told me what he really thought of me, I wanted to disappear—for the earth to open up and swallow me up. I burst into tears. I was angry but mostly I felt an intense, overwhelming feeling of shame.

"You have to stop seeing him, Sara," Andi said kindly. "He isn't a nice person."

In my hurt, crazy mind, Matteo became Florence, and Florence became ugly as a result. I just wanted to get far away from him—not to mention from a job I was really bad at. I wanted to run as fast as I could somewhere, anywhere where I could start over again. I swore I would lose weight. I would go on a diet the next day. I was never going to be treated like that again.

Once Andi decided she wasn't going to stay in Florence with Antonio, she began making plans to return to the US. I quit my job with Jacopo's family. I had made friends with some of the students from the second LFC art history program who were spending the winter in Florence. I arranged to meet one of them, Janis, in Barcelona. We would visit Formentera, where I had heard there were lots of hippies. We set our date of departure. It was my next move, the next promise for a cure. I was off and running on the search for the next magic place that would transform my life for the better.

Formentera is the smallest of the four Balearic Islands off Barcelona. In 1970, there was one ferry a day to and from the island of Ibiza. I met Janis at the port in Barcelona and we hopped on the noon ferry. In Ibiza, after buying a few staples, we set off on a thirty-five minute ferry ride to Formentera.

At that time, Formentera was basically a barren island still trying to survive after World War II. There were isolated, lonely, wide expanses surrounded by a breathtaking ocean. We landed at the one port, La Sabina, with no plans. We swung our backpacks on and started walking.

Within minutes, we were beyond buildings and out in the open on a long, narrow, sandy road. The island is so small—only thirty-two square miles—that it wasn't difficult to imagine the end, though we couldn't actually see it.

We came to a crossroads with a dusty little store that sold bread, baskets, and a few provisions.

"Let's stop and see what's around here," I said to Janis. Neither of us spoke Spanish, so it didn't occur to us to ask in the store for some suggestions. "We passed some huts that look empty. You wanna go back and look at one of them?"

Janis was tired and agreed immediately.

A few minutes from the crossroads, we found an empty stone hut surrounded by tumbleweeds and dirt. There was nothing in it, not even a door. It had probably been used for storage at some point.

"This is cool," I said. "We can sleep here and use the café at the store for a toilet and washing." We threw down our sleeping bags, unpacked our few belongings, and settled in. We walked back to the store and bought some candles.

"Wow," Janis said. "How great to find this amazing pad."

This would be our home for the next four weeks.

Each morning, we walked to the little store, bought bread and pastries for our breakfast, and set about exploring the island. We saw Spaniards with dark, leathery skin, wearing hats pulled low over their foreheads and clothes that had seemingly been handed down over many generations, walking slowly with grass baskets hanging over their shoulders filled with the day's provisions. We smiled, and they smiled back with hesitation. No one in Europe was sure what to expect from their resident hippies.

One day, at the little store, we ran into an American couple.

"You must come down to our end of the island." The woman pointed south toward an area known as Far des Cap. "Everyone lives there. We're getting married on Saturday. Please come, we'll introduce you to all our friends."

So that's where the hippies were living. "Yes," I said eagerly, "we'd love to come."

"Just follow this road west for about three or four miles. You can't miss it. It'll be so much fun."

We prepared for our first social event by dropping LSD. Though I'd heard that acid punch was always served at hippie weddings, I decided this one might be different and I wanted to make sure I was sufficiently high. We walked the hour and a half laughing at our wonderful luck, though in the back of my mind, as always, was the secret wish that I was not with Janis but a boyfriend with whom I could live on an island in a lovely house.

We arrived midafternoon on a beautiful blue day, a perfect day for a wedding. Our new friend saw us immediately and came over to greet us.

"Welcome, welcome to our home!" she said, smiling. "Have some punch. There is a little LSD in it, just to let you know. Just go around and introduce yourself."

I made a beeline to the punch. I wasn't stoned enough to be comfortable around people I didn't know. I kept drinking more of it, hoping it would take instantly.

Janis and I spent the festive day seated or lying on the ground tripping. People came and went but no one made a lasting impression. I spent most of my time staring lazily, eyes locked on guests, entertaining fantasies of the perfect hippie life. And for the whole afternoon, I didn't binge. But I did allow myself to take as many cookies, sweets, and pieces of cake as I could fit in my small pack. I wasn't bingeing at that moment, but I was preparing for the next one.

When the sky started to darken, I told Janis we should go. I wasn't sure I knew where we were going, I was still very stoned. We set off at twilight and within an hour, the sky was dark with no moon and a thousand stars. Janis was petite, and so stoned she could barely walk. Plus, she had no sense of direction, so she was hopeless. I'd always had a good sense of direction but rarely called on it when stoned out of my mind.

At one point, I stopped to try to get my bearings. I forced myself to lean on memory, which is difficult when tripping. I remembered a crossroads and that we should turn left. It was so pitch black, it didn't seem much different if I walked with eyes open or closed. Most everything I was paying attention to was inside my mind. I used all the willpower I possessed and called on my inner camp counselor to find that little road to get us back to our stone hut. I was scared but I wasn't scared. I just knew I could focus enough and get us back to the hut. We wouldn't be sleeping on the side of the road. And I did it. Without talking much at all, I managed to guide us back to our little hut.

Here was proof positive that I had the willpower I'd so often been accused of not having. That night, it seemed to me that not bingeing had nothing to do with whether or not I had willpower. I could find food any time of the day or night if I had a craving. The more people kept telling me to just use willpower, the more I thought of myself as a failure, a total fat loser. This incident showed me that what was wrong with me didn't have much to do with willpower. I didn't know what the problem was, but at least I was beginning to see what it wasn't.

After Formentera, Janis went home and I hooked up with four new traveling companions who were on their way to Venice: Mark and Beate, a couple who owned a VW bus, Shelly, who was also from the States, and Bob, a vet who had just left Vietnam. In all, we ended up spending five months together. Traveling with this group had all the same highs and lows as traveling with Andi, just multiplied. I wanted to be "part of" something so badly, to belong to a group that wanted me, but I could not figure out how to do it. I resented sleeping outside the VW bus, even though I didn't own it.

As my resentments grew, my bingeing on sugar and carbs increased. When we stopped in a town and I walked by shop windows, I saw a very large woman staring back at me. I saw her everywhere I went. It depressed me and reminded me of my powerlessness. I'd go into the nearest little food store and buy whatever sugary items they stocked and vacuum it all down. Outside, when I saw the same reflection but now under the influence of the sugar, I swore that the next time I saw her, she would be thin.

By August, our little group had rented a house in Chana, on the island of Crete. The hope was that we could rest, meditate, and get back to being a cohesive group. We'd added a young Greek girl to our entourage by this point, and it proved to be our downfall. In 1970, the Greek authorities pretty much turned a blind eye to hippies as long as we stayed on our side of an invisible line—mainly, as long as we weren't blatant about drug use, and kept ourselves separate from all Greek people. As soon as Adrianna started traveling with us, her boyfriend, Dimitri, showed up to tell her to come home, followed by a member of her family, and soon the police arrived. Her well-to-do family back in Athens was not happy, and when Adrianna refused to return, the police returned several times, first threatening Adriana and then the rest of us. Finally, they decided that we were an offshoot of Charles Manson's group and acted to get us off Crete and out of Greece.

The highlight of Crete for me was meeting Dimitri. I followed my usual pattern of spending time talking with him, then falling in love with him and imagining our perfect future. When we all were booted out of Chana by the police, I went with him to his home in Athens.

Dimitri was gorgeous—tall, slim, dark, and educated. I adored him. He didn't care that I was fat. We had wonderful, uninhibited sex. I felt comfortable in my body around him. I would wrap my arms around his waist as we sped all over Athens on his motorcycle and hug him as close as I could without squeezing the life out of him. I felt wanted, and a part of a couple for the first time since the winter with Eddie two years before.

In the three weeks I was there visiting with him, we decided to live together. Dimitri was entering medical school and I would be his "hippie, barefoot girlfriend." Four months earlier, I had sent all my belongings up to Eddie's home from Florence. Deciding to live in Athens meant a trip to Amsterdam to retrieve everything I owned.

I made the trip, a full day and a half by train, and stayed with Eddie and Sasha, who'd gotten married since the last time I saw them. I had planned to stay with them the full week I'd need to pull everything together. But it wasn't pleasant. Sasha was angry all time and refused to talk to me.

"Why didn't you tell me how much you loved me?" Eddie asked me more than once. Then, one morning, he forgot to put his wedding ring back on after his shower. Sasha marched into the living room, where he and I were talking, and threw it at him, shouting in Dutch.

I was done. I packed up my backpack and left.

Eddie followed me out of their home. "You're being silly. Really, Sara, Sasha will get over it."

"What part of 'I'm out of here, I don't understand you two' don't you get?"

I didn't actually say that, but I thought it.

I was disgusted. I didn't understand, and I felt used. I spent the rest of my week at the local youth hostel.

Two weeks after leaving Dimitri and Athens, I returned to Greece with a used car I'd bought for $100 and my belongings—only to find that Dimitri had changed his mind. He no longer wanted to be in a relationship with me. He said he'd written me a letter and sent it c/o Eddie. I'd never received it.

I was heartbroken, but more than that, I felt completely broken. I was exhausted—physically, mentally, and spiritually. Andi and Janis had both gone back to the States. I had shattered my relationship with Eddie and Sasha, whatever had been left of it. I wasn't sure where Mark and Beate were, and now Dimitri didn't want me. I felt so utterly alone, and the hole inside of me was growing and growing. My constant overeating and bingeing was destroying my body. My mental gymnastics of trying to protect myself from the shame and pain of being a fat hippie weren't working. I cried and cried.

To his credit, Dimitri did not just dump me in the street. He took me up to his parents' summer home in Marathon and told me I could stay there until I figured out what to do next. But I had lost the will to do whatever adventurous thing was next. I wanted to go home. I wanted a mythical mother's shoulder to cry on. In reality, that meant going back to Princeton and my parents.

Dimitri took care of everything. He sold my car and bought me a plane ticket. He came up to Marathon almost every day and listened to me wail. It was clear he cared about me. Looking back, I think that kind, healthy people like Dimitri were able to see past all the bluster, all the fat layers, the porcupine quills that I consistently shot out at people, and saw a Sara that was curious about the world, intelligent, and even a good friend. Dimitri likely anticipated how hard it would be living with me in the present, and there is never a guarantee with an addict that all the wonderful things we wish for them will actually happen. It depends on the addict and how they choose to respond to the pain. Dimitri wasn't a betting man—at least not a man who was willing to take a risk against all odds.

8

Trying to Get By in Princeton

I was back in Princeton to ring in 1971, a brand-new year and a time for me to double down on all my hopes and dreams for a new me. On January 1, 1971, the war in Vietnam was still raging and still dividing the country. Police had killed four students at Kent State for protesting. The Beatles were no more and the Rolling Stones were the top group in the US. The hippie movement had peaked with Woodstock and the Summer of Love and taken a real blow at Altamonte. Nixon was president and becoming more and more dictatorial as he was losing control of the country. California was now the Promised Land—the place to be for sex, drugs, and rock 'n roll.

Right after the Kent State students were shot, my mother had written me a letter that I'd received while I was still in Greece. She told me I was a parasite living off the good will of others, and if I had any conscience at all, I'd try to make a difference with my life. Now I had come home from Europe, but not because I'd developed any kind of conscience. I felt so broken, and despaired of ever finding love and happiness. All I cared about was trying to find a group of like-minded people. What I wanted more than anything else in the world was to be thin and to be loved.

After three weeks in Princeton, I was starting to feel rested and ready to take up my search again. I had started calling myself a seeker.

I defined seekers as people who always sought the truth, never giving up but never content. I had to have a name for what I was doing—and it had to have a positive spin.

My parents' home was about two hundred feet from Nassau Street and walking distance to the center of town. Less than a block away was a natural foods store, a novelty at the time. Their bulletin board was a hub for people to post What's Happening index cards. It wasn't too difficult to find out what alternative things were going on. Scanning the board one day, I saw an invitation to join a new meditation group.

Did I think this was the answer? I don't think I had enough clarity to articulate any goal. But people were talking about meditation and what a difference it made in their lives. I took down the phone number, called, and was given an address and a time to show up the next day.

The following morning, I took my parents' car, feeling entitled to it, as usual. Since I'd arrived home, I'd never once asked if my mother needed it or if it was free for me to use. My father usually walked to his office at the university, and my mother worked in the upstairs office most of the day, so I jumped to conclusions, a specialty of mine.

I went to a part of Princeton that I didn't know existed. The home was single level, in a lovely neighborhood, surrounded by greenery. I could have been in the country. I rang the doorbell.

A woman opened the door. "Come in!" she said, waving me inside. She was slim, good looking, and wearing a pair of knee-high Frye boots. I fell in love with those boots on the spot. I knew I had to have them. Deep in the recesses of my crazy mind, I thought if I had those boots, I would be attractive like her.

Before the meditation started, those of us present were asked to get seven almonds. We were instructed to take the skins off of each one, eat them slowly one at a time and then to find a place in the living room to sit for meditation. I had never done any kind of formal meditation, and I was too fearful and timid to ask the attractive woman for help. I followed the instructions, peeling the almonds and trying to eat them slowly. And then all I could do was think about almonds the rest of the time I was there, supposedly meditating.

I don't remember the names of the people who owned the home. I don't remember if I ever went back. All that stands out to me are the Frye boots and the almonds. That afternoon, I went out and bought identical boots for $100 at Hulots on Nassau Avenue. My mother was appalled that I would spend so much money on boots.

Next, I went back to the natural foods store and bought a large bag of almonds. I came back to my parents' home and set up a little shrine in the room I was sleeping in. In it, I placed a valuable Buddha statue that my mother had long used as the centerpiece of a shrine she had set up elsewhere in the house. I didn't ask her permission. I peeled seven almonds, ate them, and tried to sit still.

Two minutes later, I ate the whole bag of almonds.

The shrine stayed up in the corner of the bedroom for two more weeks. At that point, my mother's patience with me—my sense of entitlement, never asking permission to use her property, my sleeping till midday (drunk on sugar), and my fluctuating ups and downs, wore her down. I would tell people for years that she threw me out of the house. She may have asked, although that wasn't my mother's way. She usually waited far too long to deal with things that frightened or bothered her and then, in anger, laid down the law. This time, the law was that I was no longer welcome in her house. I had one week to find another place to live.

I found a room for rent with an older, single woman who lived about four blocks from my parents. The bedroom was on the top floor of a typical East Coast clapboard house. I had to walk through her part of the house to use the kitchen and go upstairs to my room. My inward-looking eyeballs made it hard to observe anything, so I don't remember her name or if I actually used the kitchen or whether I was supposed to have a hot plate up in my room.

I got a job at Educational Testing Service centered in Princeton and began working my first nine-to-five job. It was awful. I didn't have the patience to start at the bottom and work my way up the ladder. Five months later, I quit and was on the road again.

In March, I heard about the Weight Watchers program for the first time. Though founded in 1963, it was still fairly new to New Jersey. The closest meeting to me was in Trenton, twelve miles away. I borrowed my parents' car, this time with permission, and found the meeting in the American Veteran's Hall. I had to pay a registration fee, a weekly fee, and then get weighed. I stepped on the scale. It read 195 pounds.

"You are in the right place," the instructor said to me, seeing the shock on my face. I was five foot six inches and hadn't weighed myself in years. "Find yourself a seat in the front," she told me. "And please stay after the meeting so I can explain the whole program to you."

She handed me a booklet but it didn't tell me much. I looked around at the dozen or so people there. Then found a seat. After everyone had been weighed, the instructor stood in front and launched into a story of her week. Everyone laughed except me.

When the meeting was over, all but two of us left the building.

"I was just like you when I first came to Weight Watchers," she told us. "I was confused. I wasn't sure whether to be hopeful or not." Then she told us her story of being fat, of trying so many diets, of finally finding WW and losing her weight.

"I feel so indebted to WW," she concluded, "and that's why I've become an instructor. But remember I'm no different than you. I used to be fat and now I'm thin. Just like you'll be."

She had my attention. She gave me a Beginners Book and told me to read it when I got home. She told us what foods we could eat and in what proportion. She had us open our booklet and showed us lists of food. "The ones on the right-hand side are 'legal' foods," she said. "That means you can have them when you prepare your meals. All these foods on the left, they are 'illegal.' Don't eat them ever while you are losing weight."

It was the first time I'd heard the words "legal" and "illegal" used for food types. It seemed ironic to me that these particular words were being used with someone like me who didn't think twice about breaking the law. But I would use those words to refer to food for many years after this.

"These vegetables listed here"—she pointed to a third list—"these are your 'free' foods. You can eat as much of them as you want." She finished by showing us the back of the booklet, where there were squares. On the first one, she had written the date and the number 195. "Each week, I'm going to weigh you and you get to watch your weight going down. You can see here that at 5'6", you will want to weigh 142, Sara." I guess she didn't realize I was born weighing more than 142.

After buying a postal scale, I left that first meeting feeling cautiously excited. Finally, someone was telling me what to do, how to do it, and when to do it. I knew this was what I needed.

The first week, I followed instructions to the tee. I lost nine and a half pounds. I was in heaven. I enjoyed the meetings. I liked the leader. She would tell us stories and give us examples of how to get through different kinds of situations. She didn't talk about the future when one reached goal weight. As far as I knew, I just had a weight problem. All I had to do was take the weight off and everything in my life would be okay. No one said or seemed to know any differently. There were probably other people in the room who ate compulsively, like I did, but no one was talking about that. I wouldn't hear the term "food addiction" or "compulsive eating" until many years later.

I've often wondered how many of us addicts sat in the room at those meetings, hoping and praying this was the answer and that the terrible, insatiable beast inside us would be felled once and for all. Under the illusion that all my problems would disappear once I was a normal weight, I began wandering the streets of Princeton and buying different kinds of "natural foods" that I could have once I had reached my goal weight. I bought a sesame seed bar with honey in it because I'd never eaten something like that before. I put it in the drawer of my bedside table, where it sat for a couple of weeks calling my name. I never once forgot it was there.

I was lying in bed one night after I'd lost fifteen pounds. I patted my tummy, happy that I was losing weight. Then I felt a bone. It was my left hip bone. I had never felt my hip bones; I wasn't conscious I had any. I didn't exist below my neck. Once in a while, I'd see myself in mirrors or storefronts, but in those situations I was always fully dressed. At home, I only had the mirror above the sink. I'd stare at my face and wish I had a ski-jump nose like my mother. My eyebrows were so thick they almost touched. In high school, I had slept on huge hair rollers, trying to straighten my hair. I was constantly trying to improve everything above my neck. But below, I didn't look, didn't see, and therefore didn't exist. Now here I was at twenty-four years old, realizing for the first time in my life that I had hip bones.

Meanwhile, I had met a couple of Princeton students and started to party with them. I was attracted to one boy with blond hair, a nice physique, and an outgoing personality. But I had given up on boyfriends. I knew without a doubt that no one would be attracted to someone my size, so I felt lucky if I could make friends with good-looking boys.

I kept going to Weight Watcher meetings for a couple of months, but after the first couple of weeks, I started cheating—eating "illegal" foods and exceeding my number of points each day. On the days that I had mini-binges, I counted up the total points of that day and then tried to eat nothing for the rest of the week so that my weekly points would even out. I kept losing weight, but it tapered off. I didn't tell the leader that I was cheating, but she talked about cheating in her lectures. Then the mini-binges became more frequent, and I stopped losing weight altogether. I felt like a total failure. I dropped out.

My friends from Princeton were graduating that spring. They came up with a plan to drive out to California in a VW bus and asked me if I wanted to come along. According to the songs, everyone was happy in California. I wanted so much to be happy and after five months in Princeton, nothing was working out.

Whenever I was in my room, I remembered that sesame seed bar I'd bought and put away. Why should I wait until I was at goal weight to eat it? What harm could it do? It was as if the bar itself could talk, was calling out to me that everything would just be fine if I ate it. I could go right back on the WW plan the next day. I ate it. And wanted another. I was bingeing again within days.

I was back into the hell of eating. All I could think to do was get out of town and start over again somewhere else. The beast was loose, and I was running.

9
Berkeley

Berkeley in 1971 was exactly as advertised to those of us who identified as young hippies. Nothing seemed weird at all—in fact, Berkeley seemed liked one of the nicest places on earth. People were kind. When crossing the Bay Bridge to San Francisco, it wasn't unusual to learn that the person in front of you had paid your toll. Hippies hung out at Golden Gate Park all day until the park closed at dusk. There was music everywhere. The Grateful Dead played at Winterland Ballroom almost every weekend. And yet there was also a violent underground that was growing in strength, though most of us wouldn't know it until later in the decade.

The VW bus trip from Princeton was smooth at first, but by the time we were halfway there we couldn't stand each other, and I couldn't wait to part ways once we got to Berkeley. I had started Weight Watchers a second time just before the trip but was unable to stick to it. I didn't even make it all the way to California before I was full-out bingeing, buying huge bags of cheap cookies at grocery stores and eating the entire time we were en route. My sick brain still convinced me that if they couldn't see me eating, I was getting away with it. Every time the car stopped, I'd jump out, find somewhere no one could see me, and stuff as much into my mouth as possible. I'd barely chew at all, swallow, and do it again. If I couldn't wait till the car stopped, I'd do the exact opposite: put a bunch of cookies in my mouth and try to chew quietly while I turned my head away, pretending no one could see me. I treated the four others in the bus to ice cream whenever I could to cover up the sheer quantity of what I was eating. No method worked. There was no satisfying the voracious hunger inside of me.

By the time we arrived in Las Vegas, all five of us wanted the trip to be over. I was the designated driver to get us past the last part of our trip; with sugar flooding my system and feeling that Berkeley and a new life was close at hand, my anxiety level shot up sky high. All I wanted to do was get there. Beam me up, Scottie. There was a familiar, aching feeling in my gut that something couldn't happen fast enough. I was completely unable to be in the moment. It was similar to a craving. My insides churned. They hurt and just got worse with each passing moment. I felt a propulsion that seemed out of my control; I had to be somewhere else, and it had to be NOW.

I completely gave in to this feeling that possessed me. I felt victimized. Just more feelings I couldn't understand. It never occurred to me to try to understand them. To the outside world, I probably acted like a person possessed. To a therapist, I was probably having a full-blown, sugar-ignited anxiety attack.

I was looking forward to seeing Georgia, my high school friend, but I also knew that Cooper, a boy I'd had an on-and-off again crush on in college, was living somewhere in Berkeley. While at LFC, I'd been too embarrassed to let him know of my crush, so we'd become good friends and stayed in contact after graduation. On this miserable cross-country trip, I consoled myself with daydreams of our falling in love with each other. As I sped from Nevada into California, I used those fantasies as an attempt to distract myself from my anxiety.

After we'd passed the east side of the Sierra Nevada mountain range and crossed over the mountains via Tuolomne Pass, we descended into California. The drive through the upper part of

Yosemite National Park in the autumn, when winter is just starting to spread out over the tips of the mountains and autumnal color is in all the trees, is beautiful. The air itself is clean and brisk. Anyone who has ever visited Yosemite in the fall leaves enchanted and mesmerized by its beauty. There were no crowds that October of 1971, nothing to prevent one from being captivated at this first sight of California. But I saw none of it. I was too laser-focused on getting to Berkeley and starting my life anew.

In my mind, I had arrived in the Promised Land. Georgia, living right in the center of Berkeley, was in the middle of it all. Her boyfriend, a drug dealer, lived in the Haight-Ashbury neighborhood of San Francisco. Interesting hippie-type people came in and out of her house at all hours of the day.

Georgia herself was slim, a bit mysterious, and had an interest in most everything. We shared a love of art; she wanted more than anything to paint. She'd been in California for four years by the time I arrived, and the way she had set up her life, with so many people looking up to her, gave me the feeling of being in the presence of royalty.

Her home was exactly how I'd pictured hippie homes in California would be. Colorful Indian material was thrown over her sofas and chairs. She had pillows with little mirrors on them on the couches and on the floor. The windows had crystals hanging from the center beam. The light hitting the crystals threw rainbow shades of color around the room and the windows themselves were constantly twinkling.

I was in awe. I had never seen anything so wonderful in my life. Berkeley Way, Georgia's street, seemed a haven for us East Coast transplants.

If you saw a photo of Georgia and me in those days, you would see that she was slender and I was large. She was attractive, in her long skirts and flowing blouses, and I was just plain fat in whatever I wore. On me, clothes never had the desired impact—nothing like what I saw in my mind's eye when I was considering a purchase. Having failed at Weight Watchers yet again, and so recently, I was headed back up to 190 pounds. According to the Weight Watchers chart, I was at least fifty pounds overweight.

I was taking lots of drugs, but never anything that required a needle. Being an addict addicted to *more*, I probably would have overdone something that would have killed me if I had, but I was deeply afraid of needles. So I mostly smoked marijuana and hashish. I adored LSD. Georgia turned me on to cocaine and taught me how to make huge cigarette-looking things with tobacco, hashish, and cocaine all rolled up together in cigarette paper. Though I had started taking drugs medicinally, I was now stoned on something most of the time. But nothing was helping with weight control at all and the drugs just made my mood swings worse.

After staying with Georgia for a couple weeks, I found my own place—a classic concrete two-bedroom house two blocks down Berkeley Way from her. There were two exotic bird of paradise plants in the front yard, distinguishing it from the other houses on the block. It was the winter of 1971 to 1972, and I felt like the newbie in Hippie Disneyland.

The drugs did help me numb out what I couldn't control—my food intake and my weight. I couldn't understand why Weight Watchers didn't work for me. I would feel suicidal, then get stoned and look for the next thing to solve my problem. In desperation, I tried hypnosis a couple of times, as well as encounter groups, which were taking the country by storm. At those meetings, we sat in a circle, naked, and received teachings on how to love our bodies. Each time, I felt stupid and pitiful. One of the group leaders was larger than me, and seemed happy. But I had so much self-hatred that the idea of loving my body was like learning Swahili, and I knew deep inside that it would never happen. How could one possibly go from the intense self-hatred I had to loving the very thing I was convinced caused all my misery?

When I was around Georgia, my desperation to be thin intensified. I loved Georgia and treasured our friendship, but in her presence I escaped into some kind of wishful thinking. *If I could be thin like her*, I told myself, *everything would be perfect. Someone would love me, I would be happy.*

Within the first weeks of arriving, I had successfully tracked Cooper down. He was in the navy, stationed at Mare Island. In college, he had sworn to go to Canada or do something else revolutionary to avoid the draft. But when his lottery number came up as number twelve, he'd found he didn't have the courage to oppose his father, who felt the patriotic thing to do was to serve in some capacity in the US military. So he'd enlisted in the Navy. As it turned out, he would be spending his entire four years in the Bay Area. He'd rebelled a bit by refusing to live on Mare Island and when I found him that autumn of 1971, he was living in an apartment on Grove Street (now Martin Luther King Jr. Way) with a roommate, a gay man named Richard.

Coop, to me, had always been extraordinary. Other than not being willing to oppose his father, he went his own way with most things. He was tall and very thin. He had a head of thick black hair, and I always thought he looked like a handsome Abe Lincoln. He was interested in most things, especially music and making things with his hands. He had a tremendous curiosity about people and liked most everyone. I adored him, and I know he liked me. I think I'd grown on him in the first few months we spent together. Georgia used to say that the two of us were the only sane people she knew. I hung on to those words when I felt especially crazy. I didn't feel sane much of the time.

As much as I wanted to, I wasn't able to follow my craziness down any roads with no ends—which, in the long run, probably helped save me. I was trying hard to manage my life but also wanted to maintain my illusion of freedom: that I didn't have to work when, in fact, I had no idea what I was good at or what I would do for work or a career. Coop and I were a good fit this way because he had no idea what he would do when his time in the Navy was over.

We spent all our time together, and eventually he moved into my place on Berkeley Way. We were a couple. I was in a relationship with someone who loved me, and we were living together, something I'd always dreamed of. We rented out the other bedroom to another couple and also the front entryway to a Cal student. Later I wondered how we could stand it? But it was the times. We wanted community more than individual space.

Coop loved to explore, and he owned a car. We spent hours getting to know the beaches in Marin County. On weekends, we took picnics and Frisbees to Golden Gate Park, got stoned, and played all day long. We lay down under the rays of warm sun with the hundreds of other hippies there.

Sometimes, I'd rise up on my elbow and stare at the thin girls around me. Their arms would be wrapped around a boy and both would be swaying to some internal music only they could hear. *What would it feel like to be thin like that?* I'd ask myself. I'd watch other boyfriends put an arm around a shoulder and pull a thin girl close. No one had ever done that to me, not even a parent. Everyone in the park seemed to be paired up, in love, and so affectionate. *What would that kind of love and affection feel like?* Did Coop secretly wish he was with someone who looked like one of those other girls?

Sometimes I'd start crying when I had these thoughts, but more often I just stayed in my stoned, zoned-out state up in my head, wondering what-if. Sometimes I'd pray for help. Sometimes I'd promise myself I would diet. That would last until the munchies hit. I couldn't tell Coop any of this. He was always so honest with me. What if he said yes, he'd rather be with a thin woman but he loved me?

That spring of 1972, I got a letter from the Peace Corps saying I had been accepted conditionally. I had applied over a year earlier and, not hearing back, totally forgotten about the application. The letter requested that I come to an informational meeting in Denver, talk to representatives of the Peace Corps, and learn about the country I was to go to: Thailand. By the end of the weekend, I was supposed to have enough information to decide whether I wanted to join up or not.

I went to Denver. The Peace Corps held a particular appeal to me. It was a way of making money but not really being a part of the American rat race. At the time I applied, I saw it as my solution to not really wanting to have a job. I also was drawn to going back on the road.

But on my way home from Denver, I decided I wanted to stay in Berkeley with Coop. All my life I had just wanted to be loved. Coop and I seemed to be growing into a loving relationship. I didn't want to mess that up. I was good at messing up any kind of relationship. Plus, I liked California. I liked having a home that was so far away from my parents. For the first time in my life, I didn't think that taking a geographic would solve my weight problem or any other problem.

Though I'd made my decision to not go, I didn't have enough confidence to tell Coop why. I was tortured by the belief that if he knew how much I loved him, he would leave. The next day, I wrote a letter to the Peace Corps thanking them and declining the offer. Meanwhile, I wasn't kind to Coop. I loved loving him. I felt incredibly fortunate that he seemed to love me. Our being a couple made me feel more security around other people. We went to more Grateful Dead concerts than I could count. I wasn't working, so staying up late any day of the week was what I did. I was so centered on me that I would take it personally if he fell asleep in a movie or a party. I thought he didn't care enough about me to stay awake and share with me after the event was over. It was as if every little thing was a test that he didn't know he was taking. I would pick fights with him frequently, telling him he should stay awake.

Many years later, on a return trip from Seattle, I stopped in Oregon where Coop was living.

"I was pretty bitchy to you back then, Coop," I told him. "I just couldn't conceive of your life in the military and living with me in Berkeley. Talk about schizophrenic. I really don't know how you put up with me as long as you did."

"Are you implying our problems were your fault?" he asked.

"Well, yes, kind of," I admitted.

"Don't you remember how depressed I would get, Sara? I was dealing with a lot of issues of my own. I didn't tell you."

I was stunned and a bit relieved to hear him say that. I realized I'd always thought of him as a perfect being, so all that was wrong had to be about me and my not being good enough. I had asked him to jump through so many hoops, and everything was based on an insane thinking pattern. It was something for me to see that it was a two-way street. He was human and had his own issues; I wasn't the only one who had contributed to our problems.

"I don't remember. Here I am, apologizing for what I do remember, and there was so much more I didn't see at all." I shook my head. There is so much hidden in relationships.

"I think that's okay," he said. "Just as long as you know that our problems were the fault of both of us."

Coop could be very reassuring.

In June of the first year I spent with Coop, I went back to Vermont and the summer camp I loved so much to be the Counselor-in-Training Director. Though I'd made a negative impression in my teen years, I'd kept in touch with the people who ran the program, and now they were giving me another chance.

Coop helped me buy a little Datsun. I found another person to do the drive with me. With the help of lots of speed, we made the trip in three days and two nights.

Coop was a working man with normal working hours. He could request only a certain amount of vacation time during the year. So we made plans to hike in upper Yosemite after I returned.

I was gone ten weeks. I gauged how much he missed me by the phone calls I got. Another test. I didn't get enough for my satisfaction.

"Why don't you call me more often?" I asked him one Sunday.

"I don't know," he said. "There just aren't enough hours in the day. Work has been demanding."

I felt so abandoned by that response. If he loved me, he'd want to call all the time. "Can't you try harder? Every Sunday evening, maybe?" I pleaded.

"Maybe, we'll see."

Self-doubt riddled me. And there was nothing I could do. The phone was the only means of communication I had. Short on patience and long on anxiety, I resorted to ice cream from the industrial freezer underneath the eating commons. So many summers I had stood at that freezer, stuffing my face. Just like any drug, it took more and more sugar to numb out the feelings of powerlessness and self-hatred.

The camp had changed directors in the years since my childhood. I found Winnie, the present director, easy to talk to. For some reason

I couldn't fathom at the time, she had faith in me—confidence that I could be the counselor she thought of when she looked at me. Her seemingly unshakable belief in me helped me hold my head higher, and be more responsible. I loved working for her, and she made me want to be a good counselor.

That fall, after I got back from camp, Coop's friend and ex-roommate, Richard, decided to tell me that another woman had moved into my bed while I was in Vermont. She was gone before I got back, so I wouldn't have been the wiser.

I wasn't really shocked. People were sleeping around in the early '70s, and at least that explained the lack of phone calls over the summer. But it did shake my sense of security. "But he chose you, Sara," Richard said. "She's gone."

That didn't make me feel better. I went on a whopper of a binge and, for the millionth time, tried to stick my finger down my throat and vomit. I was learning about bulimia and I envied bulimics the ability to eat and eat and eat, then go to the bathroom and vomit it all up. But I just couldn't do it.

Someone had told me about ipecac syrup, which was given to babies to make them throw up. Barely able to walk, I asked Coop, "Please, can you go to the free clinic and get ipecac? I'm so sick I feel like I'm going to die."

"You're not going to die, Sara. I'll do it but I'm not happy about it."

I was convinced this was the answer. I paced the house, waiting for him to return.

Two hours later, he came back. "There was no one there when I got there, I had to wait. Then they quizzed me about why you needed it. Did you know ipecac is a poison?"

Did I care? Just give me the damn syrup.

"I had to convince the guy you had swallowed some noxious stuff. This isn't meant for adults, Sara. Do *not* ask me to do this again." He handed me the syrup and left. *Well, don't go sleeping with other women!* I wanted to yell at him.

I drank the entire bottle. It was horrible. Like drinking swamp water.

Nothing happened. No vomiting, no help. I just felt horrendous mentally and physically, wanted to crawl in my bed with the covers over my head and pray to die. That all-consuming feeling shut out everything that was good in my life.

Coop and I carried on, and that fall I found the strength inside of me to go back to Weight Watchers and try again. I didn't know what else to do. I felt completely lost and hopeless about my weight.

I stuck with the program this time. I did what they told me to do. I didn't rewrite the rules to fit my broken idea of how things should work. And I began losing weight. I lost a lot of weight. Even I thought I looked pretty.

It had been years since I had been thin. Losing weight gave me a feeling of being in control, of having strength. But there was a loophole in the Weight Watchers program. The plan told me that there were "free" foods, meaning foods I could eat any time of the day and as much as I wanted. Clearly, it wasn't designed with a food addict in mind. The Weight Watcher lecturer gave us a recipe for cabbage soup with a tomato juice base. I could put as much and as many "free" veggies in as I wanted. So every day, I made huge amounts of cabbage soup—and every day I ate it all, grazing on it all day long. I was still bingeing, but Weight Watchers was telling me that it was okay as long as I weighed my regular meals. Which I did. I also farted all day long.

Coop said I was difficult to live with. But he made a joke of it, calling my farts "rocky mountain barking spiders," and we'd both laugh. Ha ha! I was getting thin, but I couldn't go anywhere because I was still bingeing on "free" foods and now farting. I was fooling myself by thinking I had some control.

Coop and I moved to a new place together on Spruce Street. No more roommates. Just him and me. We lived on the top floor of an old redwood Berkeley home that had been divided up into apartments. I was happy there. Both the bedroom and the living room had slanted ceilings. There was a small kitchen with a table that just fit two people. Coop and I spent a lot of time at that table. He developed a new hobby: cooking. We would go out to dinner and if he enjoyed his food, he would spend hours over the stove and the counter, trying to replicate it.

That kind of determination to accomplish something was foreign to me. I was completely in awe. I wanted instant gratification or I didn't do it.

Coop completely supported my dedication to Weight Watchers. Together, we would try to figure out how I could eat some of his creations. I didn't like cooking, but with his help I learned to make meals that I liked and were satisfying. I genuinely thought I was cured. It seemed easy. I was a star in the WW program, as I'd lost fifty pounds. I had loving support from my boyfriend and I felt "popular." I loved dressing up to go to weddings or parties and show off my new body.

I was so happy. I never thought about what would happen if I stopped being happy. I think it would be fair to say that I strutted around in my world with little caution, little humility, and complete certainty that this newfound joy would last forever.

I went back to Vermont the following summer, despite my concerns about what Coop might do while I was gone. I had gotten positive

feedback from the campers, other counselors, and Winnie, the director. She'd actually grown to rely on me, and I liked her and respected
her hugely.

One afternoon, after camp was over and the campers had gone
home, Winnie and I sat and talked in the apple orchard and I told
her that I was depressed. Other than being with Coop, I wasn't looking forward to going back to Berkeley. I knew something was wrong
and didn't want to face whatever it was. I was starting to feel the
satisfaction of a job well done in Vermont—something I had had no
familiarity with since I was dedicated to not working. Out of the blue,
she suggested that I consider going to graduate school.

"You are a good counselor, Sara," she said to me. "You have natural skills and you relate to the campers. You might consider building
on those skills."

I had never considered going to a counseling program. I didn't
even know they existed. She was unlocking a whole new world for
me. It had never occurred to me that one could do in the winter what
one loved doing in the summer.

"What would I have to do?" I asked her. I was genuinely lost.

She was so kind and didn't belittle me for not having any tools for
looking ahead and thinking about my future. "When you get back to
California, do some research. Find out what kinds of counseling programs are available and what you would have to do to get into them."

"I can do that," I told her. And just like that, I had a project, a goal,
and my depression began to lift.

She smiled. "You'll keep me informed of your progress?"

I knew she wasn't just saying it. She wanted to know. She also
wanted me to return the following summer and lead the CIT program again.

Back in California, I looked around me and knew what was
wrong. Being a hippie, seeing the Grateful Dead concerts, and being
a Deadhead—living the life of drugs, sex, and rock 'n' roll—had

reached its limit with me. I was bored. I was still taking a lot of drugs and LSD on a weekly basis. Coop and I went to music concerts all over the Bay Area every week. During a concert, all was right with the world. But the concerts always ended, the drugs always wore off, and I always ended up unhappy again. If I had been paying attention, I would have noted that being thin didn't make all my problems go away.

I decided to take Winnie's advice and did some research on graduate schools in psychology and counseling. But I had no faith in my abilities and was so lazy that I kept my research to a minimum and in the end applied to only one school. I kept all of this a big secret from the people in my world, except for Coop.

In order to have my application considered and accepted, I had to take two undergraduate courses. I started at California State University, East Bay. In a complete upside-down state of affairs, I would sneak out of our home, take Coop's car (with his permission!), drive down to Hayward, and go to school. Only later did I see the irony. My need to be liked and to fit in, not to make any waves if possible, was so strong that I sold my intellect down the river. I didn't want anyone to know that I was considering going back to school for a degree. This was the time when we all believed that you couldn't trust anyone over thirty years of age. We hippies were going to change the world. Yet the dark side had already surfaced. Patty Hearst had robbed a bank near me and had gone underground. The house on the corner turned out to be the home of a group similar to the Weathermen, one of the most violent groups to emerge during this time. The house was filled with guns. Our make-believe world of love and peace no longer existed.

In spite of myself, I was making a good decision. I was making sure that I had a place to land when the world of hippiedom no longer worked for the majority of us. I just didn't know it. All I knew was that I was terrified people would find out that I wanted to go back to

school, that my mind was hungry for more, and that learning satisfied a deep need in me. Fate or some power greater than me seemed
to be taking care of me, doing for me what my crazy addict brain
could not do.

I had lost weight, but I had in no way changed my thinking or my
behavior. I still didn't know how to cope with life just as it was—or,
as some of my friends say, "life on life's terms."

10

Graduate School

I was so surprised to discover that I loved learning. I was thriving in my two undergraduate psychology classes. I arrived on time, and I studied hard. I brought my Weight Watchers lunch, packed up in a paper bag, and basked in the academic ambiance. The classrooms looked like any college classroom, the chairs were uncomfortable, and I never got to know any of my younger classmates. But I loved it.

When I wasn't accepted into the one master's program I had applied to, I quickly saw how foolish I'd been to "put all my eggs in one basket." I sadly told my professor. He asked me for all my application materials, wrote a reference, and handed everything over to the master's program in counseling psychology at Cal State, East Bay. I had been too snotty and arrogant to ever consider a no-name place for anything more than required courses.

Two weeks later, I was accepted into their program.

Cal State, East Bay in the city of Hayward, completely funded by the state of California, was part of a vast system of nine universities traversing the entire state. It was one of the best state educational systems in the country at the time. Though very successful at educating California residents, it wasn't prestigious at all. In fact, until I looked for places to take my two courses that would make me eligible to apply to graduate school, I'd never heard of it. The university and the city of Hayward are twenty miles south of Berkeley. I had never been there prior to that spring. My whole world had been the hippie communities of Berkeley, San Francisco, and Marin County.

If you'd asked me back then, I would have told you I wasn't at all class conscious—but the truth was, I had a very snobby academic attitude. My father was a Princeton professor. I thought all I had to do was stand in his limelight and doors would open for me. I had become one of the "entitled" of the baby boomer generation.

If that CSU professor hadn't gone out of his way to get me into the program, I would probably have found an excuse to not try harder, to not continue with my studies and found some logic to rationalize that attitude. But he did help me, and I was grateful to him. In truth, I don't know if I would have survived in a more prestigious institution—not the pressure, not the cost. There was no reason anyone would consider me for scholarship funding and the state system just had more flexibility than the private institutions. I was lucky, and I knew it.

I used my weight-loss success in Weight Watchers to write my application essay: I said I was a formerly fat person who wanted to grow in my own understanding of obesity, as well as to help others. It was true, I did want to work in a field where I could be helpful. But somewhere in my unconscious, I was begging for help for myself, too. Maybe I knew that Weight Watchers wasn't the complete answer to my weight problem. I wasn't hiding from facts; I just didn't have them.

Down the road, when I did have more facts—one of them being that I HATED asking for help—I told friends that when I went to graduate school, I was actually trying to get help by going in the back door. In saying that, I wanted to be amusing and enlightened: "See how much I understand myself now?" But I was really telling them that I wished with every fiber of my being that knowledge would be the answer for me. I'd discovered that I was good at thinking about things, studying things, and then talking about them. But it turned out that all the knowledge in the world without any actions on my part would. get me right back where I started: school-smarter but without a clue of what was "wrong with me."

To take action, I had to face my fears. My fear of failure, my fear that I might not actually be a victim in this world, my fear of laziness—that I wouldn't or couldn't do the things required of me.

I started my graduate program in September of 1973. Before classes started, I was asked to come meet with the head of the counseling program. I arrived at her office early and sat in the waiting room with another student. She was around my age, and very pretty. I couldn't sit quietly so I introduced myself with a "hi."

"I'm Carol," she replied, not offering anything more.

When I asked her if she was new to the program, I found out we had the same meeting time of 3:00 p.m. with Dr. S.

I kept pressing her for more information. I found out that she worked in Oakland as an assistant to a therapist. The therapist, she explained, also ran a school based on a creative approach to art, teaching, and psychology.

Ever Ms. Curious and always on the lookout for the "magic pill," I tried to find out more about what she was doing. I only understood enough to realize I wanted to know more. She was explaining things in psychological terms, and I'd only taken those two undergraduate courses. I didn't want to appear too ignorant, but she seemed content with her life, and I wanted whatever it was that she had.

"We have an open house coming up in October," she finally said. "If you'd like, I can make sure you're invited."

"I would love that," I responded genuinely. I had a glimmer of a life full of friends that were not part of my hippie crowd. I found a pen and a scrap of paper in my bag, scribbled down my information, and handed it to her. "Here's my phone number."

Dr. S emerged from her office at that point. She was memorably severe looking, around fifty years old, thin, and with dark, nicely groomed hair. But it was the way she held herself and the lack of a smile either in her eyes or her mouth that gave me the immediate impression of an unhappy, constricted personality.

We explained to her that we'd both been scheduled for 3:00 p.m. and had already agreed that Carol would go first.

"That's fine." She didn't thank us for giving her a solution, just called Carol in. I waited my turn.

When Carol came out, she handed me a piece of paper with her number on it, and I smiled. I'd made a friend in my program.

When I walked into her office, Dr. S, whom I found intimidating, welcomed me into the graduate program. It had been a little over four years since I had been enrolled in a school. It felt exciting, new, and liberating to be on a campus. It was a moment of complete certainty for me. Academics was in my blood. My father was still at Princeton, my mother was now teaching at Rutgers, and my sister would soon be enrolled in a PhD program at Harvard.

Dr. S explained that there were different tracks in the program and asked if I had thought about which track I wanted to follow. Carol had told me she was in the counseling psychology track, so I said I wanted that one even though it was not what I had put down in my application.

"This is considered a one-year program," Dr S said. "With your master's, you can go on to a PhD program, a school counseling program, or a licensing program to practice therapy in the state of California. We want you to take all your courses and write your dissertation by the end of this academic year. Of course, you are going to meet students who take more time than that. They are generally wives, husbands, and parents that don't have as much time as you do." She looked at me meaningfully.

"I understand," I said. "I would like to finish in one year."

She went on to tell me more specifics—choosing courses, who my advisor would be—and asked me if I had any questions. I didn't. I hadn't prepared enough in advance to know what questions to ask.

My new world felt glittery. I was thin, I was in a relationship with a wonderful man, and now I was in graduate school.

Things were going too well. I thought I understood the word "grateful;" I didn't. I didn't exhibit any gratitude for having gotten into Cal State, East Bay. (In the back of my brain, it wasn't Harvard or Stanford or even UC Berkeley.) Coop and I had been together two years by this point, and I'd forgotten how lonely I'd been, how much I adored him and wanted him to love me. My fear of leaving my hippie world was now masked as contempt for all the people in that world.

I got the invitation from Carol to attend the open house that October. Coop was busy that day, so I went by myself.

I found the address on Piedmont Avenue in Oakland. I walked in and immediately starting looking for Carol. But the person I found instead was . . . Georgia.

"What are you doing here?" I asked her. *What is going on?* I thought to myself. My head was spinning. This was my new world that I was being introduced to. Georgia was my old world. Georgia represented hippies, drugs, my misery, everything I wanted to move away from.

"This is the place I've been telling you about, Sara. I take art classes here and I've been seeing J as a therapist."

"Do you know Carol?"

"I know of her. I've seen her at the office."

"She's in my program," I said, a little dazed. "She's the one who invited me."

At that point Carol walked up to us. "You two know each other?" she asked, a surprised look on her face.

"Yes, we've been friends since high school." I felt dizzy. Two worlds had collided, and I couldn't wrap my brain cells around what was in front of me.

Carol took me by the arm. "Let me show you what we do here. Maybe it will help ground you.

"We have classes that meet in small groups. If you're truly interested, I suggest you start with Creative Behavior 1."

Did she hand me a brochure? I don't think so, but I don't remember.

"J, my boss, also sees people one on one. You are welcome to talk to her about that if you're interested."

I didn't want to. I wanted to go home. I had put so much expectation into Carol and the open house, but I wasn't sure how to feel now. I looked around me. I was standing in an old Victorian house that was basically empty. There was a large kitchen area—two rooms, which Carol told me were both therapy rooms in the daytime and classrooms in the evening. People stood by a long table laden with drinks, fruit, and crackers. They chatted away amiably. Georgia was there, talking with people I assumed she had met in her classes.

This didn't look like anything academic or hippie-ish. I was staring and I was stunned. It was as if both parts of my life were standing on either side of me, and I was going to fall into one of them if they didn't collide and crush me first. I didn't talk to people or ask any questions. I felt ten years old and wanted someone to come up and tell me what to do.

Georgia eventually saw me and came over. "What do you think?'
I shook my head slowly. "I don't know. I'm so confused. Here you
are, here Carol is, and this place looks so . . . so weird, empty. I think
I have to go home. I feel strange."

"It is a bit strange," she admitted, "but that's part of its charm. I'll
call you this evening."

I drove home wondering what had just happened. I still had admi-
ration for Carol, for the ideas she expressed in class. Plus, she seemed
happy to me. And when it came to Georgia—I admired her art. She
was very good, and even though I hadn't really been paying attention
to anything she'd told me about her classes, I had seen what she'd
been producing.

I wasn't rejecting this new place—which, I'd found out on my
way out the door, was called the Institute for Creative and Artistic
Behavior. I just didn't want to have to think about things. I wanted
to walk into a place, see white lights, and hear a loud voice say, "Sara,
this is the answer to all your problems."

That is not what happened.

In January 1974, I joined the Creative Behavior group at Georgia's
prompting. She was my touchstone, my familiar sense of being. I
trusted her, and after she told me more about her class and why she
loved it so much, that it was different than anything else she'd ever
done, I thought, *Why not?*

Every Monday evening, I went over to that empty house on
Piedmont Avenue, found crayons and newsprint to write on, sat
on a pillow on the floor, and waited for the class instruction. The
classes were slow and painful for me. I wanted something to happen,
but I certainly didn't want what was happening to be happening.
I was exposing some raw and vulnerable things—to myself and to

my classmates. I hadn't thought of these classes as therapy, but they were. I had begun group therapy. I began to feel like my nerve endings had somehow broken through my skin. I was so used to running roughshod over any feelings I had that, other than anger, I didn't even know I had any. I was that disconnected from myself.

The more discomfort that came up in the evenings, the more I attempted to be an academic wonder child during the day. Thinking I could juggle many balls in the air, I joined a writing group. I only lasted two visits, but that was enough time for me to meet a few men who seemed more exciting than Coop. I flirted with them, and even invited one over while Coop was at work one day. I was constantly comparing him to people I didn't know well but was projecting images onto. Anything to shove those nerve endings back under my skin.

One evening, while Coop and I were sitting at the kitchen table, I asked him if I could read him a story I'd written.

"Of course," he said.

It wasn't that I cared about the story so much; it was that my expectations for Coop and what reaction he would have were sky high. So, I read it, and when I finished, I expected him to say how really wonderful it was. And a few more gushy words.

"Um, I like it." He looked down at the table. That meant he didn't like it.

"Why don't you like it?"

"Well, it seems not quite real, like it's forced. I'm not good at this, Sara. You know that. It was okay."

"Can't you support me? Can't you say what's good about it?" I barely had a sentence out of my mouth and I was already screaming at him.

He got up and walked out of the kitchen.

This was becoming all too familiar. I would ask him for something, he would do his best, and I would hate it and say he wasn't supporting me. I told myself I was growing up past him. But I wanted so much from him. I was so angry with him, I couldn't even talk to him.

A few weeks later, I just left. I wasn't sure what I was doing. I couldn't seem to control anything in my life. Coop wasn't behaving the way I wanted him to behave. My Creative Behavior classes were painful and exhausting. I was flirting with men I had no interest in. My classes were fine, but that's only because they weren't very demanding. I had to change something or I would explode.

I asked a fellow student if I could stay at her apartment while she was out of town. She said yes. I left Coop a note saying we were breaking up and he needed to move out. This was the second big breakup we'd had, and about the fourth threat I'd made to him.

Away from our apartment, I could breathe again. I really thought that everything that was happening was Coop's fault.

He moved out. He found a room in a house full of other people. A week later, I moved back into our apartment on Spruce Street.

What would have happened, I wonder, if someone wise had said to me, "Sara, when you stop putting all that food in your body, when you no longer use sugar and carbohydrates to numb out, you are going to find out why you have used food all your life to avoid your life. You'll have to find other ways to cope with the immensity of your discomfort, your anger, and your rage. Don't believe everything you feel; feelings aren't facts." But no one said that to me. And I'm sure I wasn't ready to hear it. In spite of the pain, I told myself that I was in graduate school in psychology, and therefore, I had answers.

Within days of moving back to the apartment, I started bingeing. It had been over a year and a half since I'd binged regularly, but now it was as if I'd never stopped. This one bout was worse than ever. I

could not stop eating. Things I didn't even like. Crazy concoctions—
mayonnaise on big hunks of lettuce and telling myself, *It's lettuce, it's
not fattening.* For weeks on end, I ate everything I could get a hold of.
I made myself sick and that didn't stop me. I cried and begged God to
help me, and then I kept on bingeing.

In March, my Creative Behavior class watched me gain thirty
pounds in one month. My shame was more pain than I could bear.
Even the excessive, round-the-clock bingeing was no longer numb-
ing me. I had gotten into grad school on the thesis that I was a formerly fat person. Now I was fat again. Well on my way to becoming
obese.

Just a couple of weeks before breaking up with Coop, I had started
waitressing at The Haven, a hippie, quick-stop restaurant housed in
an old drive-in called Mel's on Shattuck Avenue. Georgia worked
there, but had different hours than me. Available to me were home-
made bread, cookies, ice cream, granola. It was a literal drugstore for
me, the food addict. I worked weekends from 5:00 p.m. to 1:00 a.m.,
when it closed. I managed to resist the call of sugar the first three
weeks, but once the bingeing started, anything that didn't move fast
enough ended up in my stomach. I told myself I wasn't stealing. I
worked there, so it was free.

My typical work shift started with me taking speed, hoping it
would curb my appetite so I wouldn't binge. But that didn't stop anything. I was a human vacuum cleaner, scarfing up anything in my
line of sight. Chocolate chip cookies and ice cream were my drug of
choice.

A couple of weeks after my breakup, Georgia introduced me to
a friend of hers, a young Oklahoma man named Dan. We started
going out. He would arrive at The Haven a little before 1:00 a.m. After
I cleaned up, we would leave and go to a party. Already buzzing on
speed and drunk on sugar, I would get stoned on hash or marijuana or
both, drink beer, and get home early in the morning. When I couldn't

sleep because of all the sugar and drugs, I would take Quaaludes to try to relax my body so that I could rest.

This went on weekend after weekend. How I managed to keep up with my classes in Hayward again proved to me that my weight problem had nothing to do with willpower, though I didn't consciously integrate that information until much later.

One morning in May, I woke up and I couldn't move any part of my body. I lay there for a few minutes, then tried again. I still couldn't move. I was terrified. My mattress was on the floor and the telephone was right next to my head. I somehow managed to get the phone off the hook and get one hand to move. I called Coop.

"Coop, it's Sara."

"I know. Are you okay?"

"No. I can't move anything. I'm scared. I don't know what's going on." I started to weep silently. I really didn't want him to know how intensely scared I was. At the same time, I wanted him to come take care of me.

There was silence on the other end of the phone. Then, "Sara, do you think this is about all the drugs you're taking?"

"I don't know, maybe."

"I'll come over. I think you should call that therapist who teaches your Creative Behavior class and get an appointment. It might help."

"Okay . . . you will come over?"

"Yes, but it will be a while. I have to get permission to leave work."

He hung up.

By then I was able to move both my arms. I pulled myself into a sitting position.

I had hit bottom, but unbeknownst to me at the time, I was to bounce around down there for a long time. I knew I was in trouble. I

took drugs more seriously than sugar. I was willing, in my hopelessness, to do whatever Coop suggested. I called J and got a session for
later that afternoon.

By the time Coop arrived, I was standing up. He held me while I
cried and cried. I wouldn't realize that I'd overdosed for years. Yet
another episode of denial in my life that would prevent me from
being able to recover. Rather than focusing on the drugs and what
to do, I focused on Coop as the answer to my misery. I wanted to
ask him to come back, to tell him that I'd made a mistake. But I was
arrogant, and I wanted him to suggest it. I told myself it was the only
way I could be sure he really wanted to. In reality, I was scared to
say I'd been wrong or that I was sorry, to ask and be willing to hear
whatever answer came.

Anyway, Coop had had it; I had broken up with him too many
times. This time was for good. I was fat again, had clearly overdosed
on too many chemicals, and my life was in shambles. Why would he
want me back? Why would anyone want me?

In the following weeks, I saw J regularly. I bought a bed frame and
pulled my mattress up off the floor. It felt like a symbol of letting go
of the vestiges of being a hippie. I was an adult now, a grad student,
(a seriously flawed, insecure, self-hating, fat grad student, but still.)

Over the next few weeks, I started feeling comfortable again. That
wasn't necessarily a good thing for someone like me. The more comfortable I felt, the more my denial of how bad things were returned. I
was no longer motivated to make the kinds of changes I would need
to deal with my addictions. I threw all my energy into therapy, my
course work, and the beginnings of internship work. I had to pick a
subject for my thesis, but I had no idea what. Regardless, it was clear
that I couldn't finish it all by June 1974. I made an appointment with

Dr. S and told her that I could finish the coursework but would have to spend the next academic year writing my thesis. She told me to come back within the month with a subject.

The overdose terrified me. Completely ignorant, I just decided that Coop must have been right. I decided to believe him, that it had to do with all the drugs I was taking. I never did hard drugs again. But without them, my bingeing got worse. My life started to resemble a broken record. I would binge until my cravings had run their course. Once I put the sugar in my body, I seemed to have no power over when the binge would end. Maybe it would last one evening. More likely, I'd wake up "hungry" and start again. If I tried to white-knuckle it, I couldn't think about anything else. I'd get hungrier and hungrier, and then I'd give in.

Of course, my cravings had nothing to do with hunger. Even I knew that by this point. I'd ask myself, *How can you be hungry when you've just eaten four cartons of ice cream?*

In a short break from bingeing, I'd call J or another person for support. We'd come up with a plan—to start Weight Watchers again, or to find a food partner and tell her how I did each day. Once, I started a sensible diet and committed to a friend that I would sell my new dining room table that I loved if I went off the diet. Of course, I binged, and I had to sell the table.

Here I was again, for the millionth time, hating myself for being so weak, so undisciplined. I assumed that everyone I knew saw the same thing I did.

What is wrong with me? I obsessed over that question. I couldn't stand to be alone. I felt tortured by not knowing, by thinking I was cursed, by anxieties and panic I couldn't control. And still, since I needed to be with people, I put a smile on my face and pretended everything was okay.

All the evidence was building that this was beyond my control. But TV, ads, diet plans, and books all helped me keep my head in the sand because they were promising that the future I wanted was within my control. What I know now, but had no way of knowing then, was that the problem was not my willpower, or lack thereof, but the foods I was putting in my body.

Any hope of being thin again, of returning to those wonderful feelings of only six months prior, was waning. I didn't know what I wasn't doing. From 1974 to 1979, I roller-coastered in weight. When I was down in pounds, I was white-knuckling my food intake every day. When I was up in weight, I felt sorry for myself and let everyone know that I was trying so hard, but that nothing worked. Everyone had advice for me. No one in my life knew anything about food addiction. My therapy crowd all said it was a matter of self-control. They got the support part right; I wasn't going to achieve anything on my own. But the control? Even with all the support in the world, I was never going to be able to control my binges as long as I kept putting sugar and other such foods in my body. I could just as easily have gone to the beach and stopped the waves from coming in.

Meanwhile, I wrote my thesis with a lot of help from women who understood academic writing. I had been volunteering at a Women's Health Clinic in Berkeley and met some wonderful, smart, active women there. I had picked a theme for my thesis, which I no longer remember, that had to do with the work we did at the clinic. These women jumped in to help me, with ideas and guidance on making my writing academic enough for a thesis.

In June 1975, I graduated from Cal State, East Bay with an MS in counseling psychology. I began all the requirements I would need to take my licensing exam for the Marriage and Family Therapy license. My therapist became my supervisor and helped me get my needed hours. I took the exam in December of 1975 and passed by the skin of my teeth. I only know that because I was so sure I had done better than anyone else that I called the licensing office to find out. They told me I'd passed by three points. Humbling.

I entered the professional world of psychology in January of 1976. Anyone who thought I had no willpower was seriously mistaken. I needed something in order to deal with my weight and food issues, but that thing clearly was not willpower.

11

The Beginning of the End.

Having an MFT (Marriage and Family Therapist) license in 1976 in California was a bit like standing in an airport with a ticket in your hand. California graduate schools were spitting out prospective therapists by the dozens. There were far more of us graduates than there were jobs. I was told that I could leave California and get a "real" job or stay put and get a "bread and butter" job while I tried to build up a private practice. I wasn't going to leave California. It was my first adult home, and I didn't have the courage I'd had in my early twenties to start life all over again somewhere else.

After five months of pounding the pavement and getting a plethora of rejection letters, I was hired as assistant director of Student Activities and residential counselor at Mills College in Oakland. Mills was one of the few all-women colleges left in the country. I packed up my little apartment on Spruce Street and moved to the campus for the academic year of 1976 to 1977.

Nine months later, I was fired from my job.

I had no concept of being a worker among workers, of respecting the boundaries and limitations of my job description. I spent a lot of my time attempting to be every student's best friend. In Student Activities, I had the idea, which I thought was brilliant, to have Weight Watcher classes on the campus. I would lead them. Instead of going to my immediate superiors, I jumped a few rungs on the academic ladder and went to the director of Student Life. She gave me the go-ahead. When she fired me, my boss, Elizabeth, who had to be one of the kindest people on earth, explained to me that just because I came from an academic family didn't mean I could abuse the hierarchy that was required in these institutions of higher learning. If I had an idea or a request, I, just like everyone else, had to follow the normal channels: come to her first, and she would go to her boss if necessary. Being a great boss, and a communicative one, she asked me: what had been going through my mind? I couldn't tell her without sounding extremely grandiose, which was exactly what I was. I was impulsive, and when I had an idea I didn't want to wait for it to go through the normal process. I was too impatient. I didn't think through anything, certainly not what the impact of any decision I made would have on me or on others.

What Elizabeth said to me that day would stay with me for years. "Sara," she said, "if you throw a pebble in the water, the waves are going to hit every part of the shore. You can't choose."

When she heard that I had been let go (no one actually used the word fired), another staff member at Mills recommended me to a friend of hers who was director of Student Activities at the College of Marin.

The College of Marin, in Kentfield, California, was a thirty- to forty-five-minute drive from where I had moved to in Berkeley after leaving Mills. I wasn't in a position to be picky, however, and since the referral was a friend, the director hired me at the first interview. I was given the job title assistant director of Student Activities but, in fact, I was a glorified secretary. I hated the job, and I didn't like my boss.

My thirtieth birthday fell in the first month of that job. I invited

every new acquaintance I'd made to join me at a restaurant to celebrate. I barely knew anyone on that campus, but I didn't have the
wisdom to sit back, listen, and learn how things were done. I wanted
to make a big splash—wanted to be the center of their attention for
an hour or two.

Two months later, someone whose opinion I respected said to me,
"You had some kind of balls inviting us all to your birthday party and
asking us all to pay for our own meals. We didn't even know you."
Once again, I hadn't thought through the impact my actions would
have on other people and ultimately on me. Like a child on a swing, I
swung from grandiosity to self-pity and cried copiously when I fell off.

I was fired from that job within three months. It didn't once occur
to me to learn from that firing, or the one before it. I just chalked
them up to a bad fit and figured I was destined for better things.

My next job was with the American Red Cross.

In 1977, the American Red Cross (ARC) in Alameda was housed in
a beautiful Victorian mansion on Central Avenue. At that time, it
was the Red Cross closest to the Alameda Naval Air Station, and had
served Naval families, especially wives, during World War II. Now,
thirty-three years later, ARC Alameda had a staff of three people,
plus many volunteers in their retirement years, who drove the elderly
to appointments. I was to be one of the staff members.

My new office overlooked Central Avenue, a wide, tree-lined street,
on the island that is Alameda, which is accessible by three bridges.
We used to joke that if you lived in the Bay Area and wanted to go
back in time twenty years, you should cross a bridge to Alameda. My
immediate supervisor was an alcoholic named Martha. She kept a
bottle of liquor in a drawer of her desk and sipped it constantly when
she thought no one was looking.

When I interviewed for the job, I was told that I would be director of Family Services and Disaster Preparedness. Within days of starting the job, it became clear that there were no families to service. The Red Cross in Alameda was out of date.

Every Friday morning, a large batch of Mother's Cookies was delivered to our office. The Red Cross was funded by donations, and during the war and its aftermath, Mother's, a Bay Area company, had donated packages of cookies for the wives and families who came to the office to talk to a staff member or ask for help with transportation or managing a household of young ones. The war was long over, but apparently, no one had bothered to inform Mother's that the cookies were still arriving every week.

For a food addict, this was nirvana or hell, depending on the day. It was easy for me to take five, six, seven packages home every Friday—and I was being conservative, because I thought that if I took them all, someone might notice. But there was no one there to monitor me. Sometimes the packages didn't even make it to the car for me to take home for the weekend; I would start bingeing as soon as they arrived at the office.

The dance was familiar. I would try and stay away from the kitchen. But as was true for all things prohibited, the more I tried to stay away, the louder the cookies called. I'd rationalize. I'd tell myself, *I'll just go down and get a small plateful.* Five minutes later, it was another plateful. I'd then tell myself I was getting exercise running up and down the stairs. After four trips, full of sugar, I'd abandon the struggle to be sane and just grab the bags, bring them upstairs, and polish off one or two before end of the day.

There was nothing for me to do at ARC, which made the days endless. I'd ask Martha, my boss, what exactly she wanted and she'd wave her arm in the air and say, "Oh you know, visit some families. There must be some families in the books still." Naval families did live in the area, but none seemed to need the kind of help that the Red

Cross could give. I visited some of them and was invited to a variety of lunches. The Oakland Red Cross (fifteen miles away) was the center for disaster preparedness, so I sometimes drove over there to find out what they were doing. My chapter sent me on a long weekend to Arlington, Texas, to be trained in disaster services, and though I learned CPR, nothing else from the weekend would be useful in my time at the center.

So I waited for Fridays, when the cookies came in. And I started studying for my licensing exam, and homework that my supervisor gave me each week, at work. No one noticed or cared. Nothing could fill up the hours in a month. I stared at the walls a lot and ruminated on my weight and food.

I was hoping to build up a private practice so I wouldn't be beholden to these bread-and-butter jobs. I would lie and sneak off back to Oakland to see clients. When I started at ARC, I had four clients. I started scheduling them at the end of each afternoon; my day at the Red Cross officially ended at 5:30 p.m. But I'd leave at 3:00 p.m. three days a week to try to squeeze in clients until late in the evening.

By the time I left ARC, I had ten clients and two secrets: I was stealing most of the cookies and not doing any work but accepting their money. I convinced myself that I was being paid so little, I deserved to take what I could. And anyway, there was no one around who seemed to care. But if I really believed that, why was I sneaking around?

Most addicts that I know have a strong sense of right and wrong. As I was getting older, no longer doing drugs, trying to limit my intake of sugar, and no longer smoking cigarettes, that sense of right and wrong seemed more developed in me. I knew when I was doing something wrong but did it anyway. Each incident added to a growing number of rocks that I had metaphorically dropped on my soul. I could stand it only so long, and then I would have to numb out. The cookies were always available, as were twenty-four-hour grocery stores.

No surprise; I was gaining weight again. As my weight climbed closer to that original number when I'd started Weight Watchers, it became harder to sleep or to find any respite from the vicious self-talk. I was having acute panic attacks. They took the form of my insides racing 100 miles per hour, the feelings of hopelessness and helplessness paralyzing me. I'd lie on my couch or in my bed, feeling unable to move, with the four horsemen galloping all over my head, racing and racing, and me, with my sick mind, trying desperately to stop them and find yet another solution.

That spring, I saw an advertisement for a place in El Cerrito, California, just north of Berkeley, that promised fast weight loss in a month. The ad said it was a medical weight loss center. I liked the sound of that and made an appointment.

I showed up at their door late one afternoon and was greeted by a woman in a white nursing costume.

"Welcome, err . . ."

"Somers. My name is Sara Somers. I would like to know more about what you do here."

"Please, come in, sit down. Fill out this form and when you've finished, I can give you all the details." She looked extremely pro- · fessional in her whites. I wasn't sure if she was a nurse or a receptionist. She handed me a clipboard with two pieces of paper that had questions, front and back. It was the usual stuff. *Who are you? How much weight do you want to lose? Are you allergic to anything? Have you ever had the following symptoms or diseases? What programs have you already tried? If you decide to join us, please sign here to agree you won't hold us liable for anything.*

I filled out the form and returned it to her. She asked me to wait. I saw a few brochures on a coffee table and picked one up. It cited a doctor who oversaw this office, as well as a number of others. There were photos of happy, thin men and women. They were exercising or hugging each other or posed with arms around children, showing off a happy, contented family. The brochure said I would be receiving Vitamin B shots in my behind that would help suppress my appetite, give me more energy, and relieve my depression.

My magic pill was turning out to be a shot in the butt? I waited for the doctor, feeling hope—*Will this work?*—fear—*What am I doing?*—and anxiety—*How do I know these shots are really Vitamin B? How did I get so low that I'm sitting in a tiny office in El Cerrito Plaza, chasing the next magic pill?* I pushed all those thoughts away. Any sense of caution I felt, I disregarded by telling myself that I was just doing research. I would ask a lot of questions, act like I was also a professional. But I wasn't acting professional. I was desperate and sitting in a place that catered to people like me.

The "nurse" returned and told me to follow her. She walked me through a door to another room. A man, also in white garb, entered the room. After introducing himself and seeing that I held a brochure, he nodded his approval and said, "If you decide to join us, we want you to come in every morning for a shot. It won't hurt, I promise."

My eyebrows rose. A needle. What had happened to my fear of needles? Was my fear turning out to be a conditional fear dependent on the depth of my desperation?

"We will give you a food plan and want you to follow it exactly. You'll pay for a month at a time."

"What about the shots? What's in it? Why do I need to come every day?" I asked, trying with every fiber of my being to look less desperate than I felt.

"It's a combination of Vitamin B solutions. It's completely healthy. We have figured out how to combine the vitamins so that you'll have energy and won't be hungry."

Who is "we"? I didn't ask. I was too embarrassed and didn't want to appear completely ignorant. "I see," I said. "When do I let you know?"

"Well, we are having a special this week. If you join us, you get a 20 percent discount, and if you join today, we will take another fifty dollars off." He smiled.

Hook, line, and now sinker. I felt incredible pressure. I was that desperate. Nothing was working. Maybe this was a solution. Yes, it was expensive, but I felt I'd be a fool not to grab it.

"Okay," I said.

No time had passed. I was sitting duck number one thousand for people like this—people who psychologically understood how addicts were hard-wired. Don't give them a minute to think about it. He had closed the deal.

The rest of my visit went quickly. The doctor asked me to get on the scale, and noted my weight on a chart. After taking care of the finances, the nurse, if that was what she was, handed me some literature and told me to return in the morning. I didn't need to make an appointment; I would be in and out.

For the next two months, I drove twenty minutes north to El Cerrito every morning, received a shot in my butt, and then turned around and drove thirty minutes south to Alameda to work at the Red Cross.

My food plan consisted of a shake for breakfast, and for lunch and dinner some protein powder I had to buy from the medical center followed by a chicken breast with salad. They also sold me little packets of fat-free dressing.

The weight dropped off me. It was easy to do. Even the cookies, stacking up in the kitchen, as no one else was interested in them, didn't call out to me.

This was it! I had been cured. I was so happy. Not only was it working, it was working fast. My appointments lasted two minutes. I didn't ask questions and they didn't give me any more information.

After the first month, I'd lost thirty pounds. I signed up for a second month. The weight loss was slowing down, but I was fine with that. I took my hard-earned money and went clothes shopping. I couldn't stop looking at the person in the mirror. I was getting thin again—I looked pretty again! The self-hatred I'd been tormenting myself with was shut away for the time being.

I wrote to my sister—something I only did when I was thin and feeling good about myself. I told her I'd been dieting and I'd lost a lot of weight. I added some words to make her think it was a natural and healthy food plan. Two weeks later, I got a letter back from her. She didn't quite say, "you fool," but it was there. What she wrote was:

"Natural food plans will tell you to eat nuts and seeds and all the vegetables you want. Yes, you'll lose weight, but you'll probably gain it back again. The only real answer for people like us is Overeaters Anonymous. Look and see if there are meetings in your area. There must be."

Overeaters Anonymous? Never heard of it. I had heard of Alcoholics Anonymous but knew nothing about it. I thought my sister was a bit off balance and I didn't want any part of something she recommended. So I just tucked the letter into a pile where I saved correspondence, never to be looked at again.

I felt let down that she didn't share my excitement. Instead of curiosity to investigate what seemed to be working for her, I felt a strong resentment building up. *Why can't she say, 'That's wonderful'? No, she still has to tell me that she has something better.*

Was it a coincidence that Vicki happened to mention an Anonymous program now? Until that spring of 1979, I hadn't really drunk excessively since college. I had long ago decided that alcohol had too many calories and I could get just as high with drugs. But drugs were no longer an option for me. I was beginning to be more social, and most of my friends drank wine at meals and enjoyed talking about their knowledge of wine. This was a new development for me in my social life. This crowd wasn't drinking to get high but as part of a meal. And we were at the age where it seemed important to know all about wines and vineyards and what went with what. I did live in California, after all!

Even though the medical center recommended no alcohol, I was so close to my goal weight that I reasoned it wouldn't matter if I had a glass or two of wine at dinner when I was with friends.

Of course, for me there was no such thing as a glass or two of wine, any more than there was one or two nuts or one or two scoops of ice cream. It was all or nothing. Very quickly, I fell into what I would later refer to as the Alcohol Diet. I loved how wine made me feel. Since I was eating so little, it didn't take much to get buzzed. Coming home from work, I would stop at the grocery store and buy two or three bottles of wine. I used the same reasoning I had always used: *I'll have two glasses tonight and have the rest of the wine available for later; that way, I won't have to go to the store again.* I'd also like to buy a bridge in Brooklyn!

I started buying the wine earlier and earlier in the day. And my stops at the grocery store were soon for boxed wine. I had stopped caring if it was good wine or not. What I cared about was quantity, not taste. I stopped following the plan the medical center had given me and eventually stopped going for the shots.

I needed an excuse to stop, so I told myself it was far too expensive. (If I had stopped to think and compare, I would have seen that I was probably spending as much money on wine as I was on the fee the center charged me per month. But I didn't.) The center itself didn't seem to care. I never heard from them again.

With the parameters of the medical center plan gone, I drank more and ate less. For a short amount of time, I didn't gain weight, and, in fact, kept losing. And so the Alcohol Diet worked until it didn't. Eventually, I craved sugar in hard form, and as the alcohol had set off the craving for sugar, I was soon back to bingeing. I was only six months into my new diet with the shots and here I was, back into the cookies at work and buying ice cream along with the wine on my way home. I was gaining weight yet again, and now getting drunk a lot, too. My newfound happiness and confidence disappeared like smoke from a cigarette.

Desperation and hopelessness, never far away, were right back to needle me and convince me what a piece of shit I was. Over the previous seventeen years, I had tried hypnosis, encounter groups, Ayds—a caramel-type candy that was supposed to make one feel full, alcohol, Weight Watchers, amphetamines, behavioral therapy, promises to friends, the Atkins diet, the macrobiotic diet, Slim Fast, and probably many more diets or programs that now elude me. My life had become one of obsessing about my weight or food twenty-four hours a day, seven days a week. I thought about what I would eat or wasn't going to eat, I obsessed on yesterday and how I would never do "that" again and tomorrow and how everything would be different. I couldn't walk down a street without staring at myself in shop windows and despising that person whose reflection I saw. If I walked into a room of people, I knew everyone was talking about me and how fat I'd gotten. When trying to fall asleep at night with nothing to distract me, I felt tortured by the hell I was in. I still didn't know what was wrong with me, but I was pretty sure it was me—that I was a defective person and maybe it was better that I wasn't on the planet.

Finally, I remembered my sister's letter and wondered if there was in fact an Overeaters Anonymous meeting near me in the Bay Area.

PART II

Fall down seven times, get up eight.
—Buddhist saying

12

Cambridge

Between 1979 and 1983, I had four agonizing years trying and failing to manage my daily life, which was more overwhelming than it had ever been. I was attending Overeaters Anonymous meetings (a twelve-step program similar to Alcoholics Anonymous) to address the bingeing. There turned out to be plenty of meetings in the Bay Area. They were mostly held in church basements, library meeting rooms, and hospital meeting rooms, anywhere that supported the goal of OA and charged cheap rent.

Coming from a therapy background, I found it difficult to accept the notion of powerlessness. The members were telling me that I had a disease and had no power to make the disease not a disease—I could only arrest it. Now that I was a pickle, I'd never be a cucumber again. I thought that meant I was weak. I approached the program as a diet—the exact wrong way to do it. That was my goal: to lose weight. I just didn't get the rest of the program. After four years, I was feeling as hopeless and desperate as ever.

The previous four years had started with meeting a man and getting engaged. He worked in a recovery house program and I'd met him over the phone when I called asking for information about Alcoholics Anonymous. He'd invited me to coffee and given me the information he thought I needed. Then he'd asked me out on a date.

He was blond and fairly nice looking, in that rugged, well-worn Texan cowboy manner. He spoke with the requisite Texas twang that slid through doorways and could be heard rooms away. Falling in love always seemed like a good solution to my misery, but, in the end, it only brought on more. I had no comprehension how to do relationships. I wanted someone to love me and never really thought about what I had to do in return.

It turned out he didn't, either. We bumbled along quite nicely for a couple of months, decided to live together, and immediately started screaming at each other and fighting. During a peaceful period, he asked me to marry him. I said yes. Then the fighting started up again. Neither one of us was more at fault than the other by the end, but we were definitely toxic for each other. I eventually called off the engagement two weeks before the wedding. I knew in my heart that the marriage was a terrible idea. I asked a friend if I could stay in her cabin in the Sierras for a weekend to "think things over."

I was almost to the cabin in the Sierra foothills when I stopped at small food store, the last one before the twenty or so cabins that made up a small community off of Route 80. I bought necessary things but then found I couldn't leave without a full bag of brownies, ice cream, and whatever other candy and treats the small store carried—my solution to not knowing how to make big decisions. I started eating before I reached my weekend home and didn't stop for the entire weekend. I spent the weekend crying, writing, feeling very sorry for myself, depressed and physically ill from being stuffed. I was miserable. I didn't want to marry that man, but I felt guilty for breaking it off. Underneath it all, I was terrified I was losing my mind.

In July of 1979, my father stopped in Oakland on his way home to Princeton after a trip to China. For years, Americans weren't allowed to go to China but Nixon had recently opened the doors for visits. As of that summer only medical professionals were allowed in, and even then only on guided and closely watched tours. Daddy wasn't a doctor but rather someone fighting for realistic healthcare costs. He and my mother had been fighting for socialized health-care for years. They had written books on the skyrocketing costs of healthcare and the fact that a large percentage of the money was going into the pockets of the insurance companies. He should have been the enemy to many in the medical profession, but he was respected so much for his thoughts and opinions that he'd been included in this China trip.

His visit turned out to be the last time I saw him healthy. While he was there, I asked him to come to a therapy session with me, and he willingly did. I told him how much I loved him. He said he loved me very much. If he thought it was strange that I told him in a ther-apy session, he didn't say anything or make me feel less than. It felt like a very healing moment. I remember walking out the door of the therapy office feeling so good about him and me. We walked down the street holding hands on our way to dinner.

Three weeks later, driving home from Princeton University, he had a massive cerebral hemorrhage. Bad decisions were made and he ended up living for twelve years completely dependent on my mother, nurses, and caretakers for even the smallest things—like going to the bathroom. He was sixty-eight years old at the time of the stroke, younger than I am now.

At the time of his stroke, I had gone up to Mendocino with friends. The call came in the middle of the night, followed shortly thereafter by a large glass of cognac. I was in shock. I flew back to Princeton. My father was in a coma at Princeton Hospital, and I witnessed my mother, who needed to be in control of everything, at a complete loss for how to deal with this situation. I didn't recognize the fear and terror in her. I was so focused on myself and my troubles that I was no help to her at all. This only made her angrier. All my feelings of confusion, loss, powerlessness were directed at her for always being such a bitch.

I stole bottles of alcohol from their drinks cupboard and hid them in my suitcase. She found them when she searched my suitcase and threw me out of the house yet again.

Thus started many years of painful struggling with my mother. Whatever she was, I was a terrible daughter. I didn't have one ounce of sympathy for her. I would come to Princeton a couple of times a year and want to be with my father. She had redesigned the downstairs as a hospital room so my father could live at home, and when I was there, she'd want me to relieve the nurses of their duties. I was furious she would expect *me* to take over nursing duties on my vacation. This polarizing struggle went on until my father died.

A couple of weeks after my father's hemorrhage, I quit my day job at the American Red Cross to start a business of my own. I had the support of my mentor and supervisor but my full-time focus on food and controlling my calorie intake prevented me from grasping what a huge decision that was. It would be fair to say that during that entire summer, I never let any feelings get far enough in that I actually felt them. I just binged or dieted and stayed in total denial about how unmanageable my life was getting.

I wrote to my sister a couple of times to tell her how badly I was doing at this OA business. We wouldn't find out until years later that the OA meetings I was going to in California were very different from the ones she was going to in Cambridge.

Now it was 1983, and I was dating a new guy, Peter, who I'd met in AA. I had originally gone to AA because it was a complete mystery to me how OA worked and what the twelve steps were. I soon realized

I probably belonged in AA. But I chose to use it as a social scene. I didn't learn much about the program of recovery but did see that there were a lot of good-looking men in AA. So, even though I was attending these meetings that promised me I'd stop bingeing, I kept on eating.

In desperation that summer, I decided to fly east to see my sister, but it was under the guise of visiting my parents in Princeton for their thirty-seventh wedding anniversary. I needed to see for myself what these meetings were like that she was attending.

It was late August, and the plane was hovering over Logan Airport.

"We are not cleared to land," the captain told us over the speaker. "I can't tell you any more than that except to say that I will keep you posted."

No, no, no, I wanted to scream at someone.

Feeling captive in my window seat and powerless over whether we would land soon or not, I reflected on the last four years since Vicki had suggested I attend Overeaters Anonymous. I hadn't attended a single meeting until six months after she told me about it; in my usual, stubborn way, I'd resisted any advice from her. Even when I finally had gone, I'd told myself I was just doing research for my profession.

I didn't like OA, I didn't understand OA, but I didn't know where else to go. I went to meeting after meeting trying to figure it out on my own. I didn't tell anyone except my therapist how confusing I found it. I was terrified of being thought weak.

Over the four years I had been going to weekly meetings, I'd gotten to know lots of people. My priority was to get thin more than to change my lifestyle, so I hung out with the thin people at the meetings, hoping that whatever they did would rub off on me. I went to meetings in Berkeley, Oakland, and San Francisco. A typical meeting would run an hour and have anywhere from five to thirty people show up—most feeling desperate like me, all seeking a solution for our disorder. Nothing seemed to inspire in me the same feelings that Vicki felt about her Cambridge OA.

The plane continued to circle Logan Airport. I was a ball of nervous energy. My body buzzed with anxiety. I couldn't do anything but sit, look at the clouds, and think. My leg bounced up and down, my heart beat far too fast, and I felt crazed. I was exhausted from six hours of feeling extreme feelings and sitting there hugging my knees and struggling to calm down. I wondered what was going on that we couldn't land. We were so close, but that meant nothing. It could take another two hours before we learned what was going on and when we were landing.

Finally, we landed in Boston. I felt like I had regained some control.

Yet, I had no plan at all. I would be staying in a hotel that night and seeing Vicki the next day. I had some porcelain pieces that had been left to Vicki by our grandmother. I was delivering these to her and she was going to take me to one of her meetings. Three days later, I would turn thirty-six years old. After the two-day Cambridge visit, my boyfriend, Peter, was going to fly out to meet me, and we were going to drive down to Princeton together.

Vicki and I still didn't get along well, and I did wonder briefly what had gotten into me that would put me under the delusion that this time it would be different. But I had my goal, and that superseded any intelligent thoughts I had. I had asked her if she would take me to one of her meetings that she claimed were so different from mine. If she was ambivalent about taking me, she didn't show it.

I met Vicki the next day in Harvard Square. She took me to a 5:30 p.m. Friday OA meeting. We walked inside one of those stately brick buildings of academia that fills one with awe at the knowledge and wisdom that have passed through their halls. *Why couldn't I be smart enough to attend Harvard?*

I took a deep breath as we walked into the meeting.

Even though Vicki had told me her meeting would be different from what I was used to, I wasn't prepared at all for what greeted me. At first, I didn't know why. I felt a mixture of fear, curiosity, and anxiety—fear because I wanted an answer so badly and the pessimist in me knew I'd be disappointed; curiosity because Vicki had written enough about what she was doing that I wanted to see for myself; and anxiety because I still wanted to walk into a room and have everyone like me. Here in Cambridge, I wanted people to think, *Oh, that's Vicki's sister. She's so cool.*

I walked into the room full of my tangled emotions, expectations, and hopes. Glancing around, I was immediately intimidated. These people were thin; it seemed like they glowed. Vicki and I sat down, me close to the door in case I wanted to get out fast.

I listened while a women told us her eating history, ugly like mine.

"I went to my parents' home this weekend," she added. "They kept asking me when I was going to eat normally. My mother was embarrassed to have me at her table. But I'm here to tell you that even though I was so upset with her, I didn't eat over it. I absolutely didn't eat no matter what happened." She was radiating a sense of the miraculous.

I was stunned. In my four years in OA, I'd never heard anyone talk like this. Back in Oakland, my mind would often turn off and I'd slip into daydreams. Most of the people in the meetings I attended were overweight, and I didn't want what they had. During those four years, I'd never known what to do or not do because I wasn't taking it seriously. I'd been desperate to stop bingeing and gaining weight, but I hadn't had enough respect for the meetings or the program to pay attention. I'd all but given up on a cure for bingeing; it was the friendships that had kept me returning to those rooms.

Sitting three thousand miles from Oakland, next to Vicki, I knew immediately that something very different was happening in this room. This was not a social club. These people were here to talk about recovering from a food addiction, and outside issues got left at the door. It was straight talk and it was hopeful. These were happy people. They knew that stopping bingeing was not in anyone's individual power. There was commitment, love, gratitude, and togetherness in that room.

Impressed as I was, I wasn't going to let my sister know it. I hid behind my intellectual snobbery. When she asked me what I thought afterward, I said, "It was okay."

"Good," she said, "I'm glad it was useful."

My sister was thin again, and I was jealous. My sister was getting her doctorate at Harvard, a place I couldn't have gotten into even in my dreams. My sister had found a solution before I had. I put a spin on the Groucho Marx quote, thinking to myself that I wouldn't belong to any club that would have Vicki in it.

I met Peter in downtown Boston, and we left for New Jersey the next morning in his rented car.

Peter was tall and handsome, and I loved flirting with him. I thought he was very sexy. We got along well. We enjoyed movies and doing silly things together. He had two young children from a previous marriage, and he'd once taken all three of us to Disneyland. We'd had a wonderful time. As long as I didn't ask too much of him in the way of emotional support, we did well together. Planning this vacation, I'd thought a car trip with him would be wonderfully fun.

By the time we got together in Boston, though, I was already on the cusp of a huge binge. And the more I held my emotions in, the worse I felt.

We took the Massachusetts Turnpike to the New York Thruway, headed to New York City to celebrate my thirty-sixth birthday. Somewhere in the Hudson Valley, I wanted food—more specifically, sugar. What overcame me in that moment can only be described as being possessed by obsession. I couldn't think about anything else. I didn't see any of the beautiful landscape that so many artists over the years have come to paint.

"I have to go the bathroom," I told Peter, desperate for food and not knowing what else to say to get him to stop the car.

"Sure," he said. "But the next stop is about ten minutes away. Can you make it?"

I could and I did but those ten minutes felt like ten hours, one minute after the other ticking slowly as my cravings became more insistent.

He pulled into the rest stop and, as he got gas, I went to the accompanying fast food store. I bought chips and cookies and Mars bars and my favorite, Snickers bars.

Back in the car, I tried to act normal. I tossed the bag on the backseat and joined Peter in the front as before. I casually reached behind me with my left hand to get stuff out of the bag, but I couldn't reach it. I leaned over more and still couldn't reach it. I felt crazed. My drug was so close, yet so far. I felt like a junkie plotting how to get my fix without letting my boyfriend know how badly I needed it. I was too ashamed by the intensity of my craving to unbuckle my seatbelt and reach over the seat and grab the bag and bring it up front.

"I don't feel well," I finally said. "Pull over. I think I should lie down. It's easier on the backseat." Another lie.

"Should we stop again and get you some medicine?"

"No, no, I just need to lie down. I'm sure I'll be okay later."

"You're the boss."

Ha. If only he knew who the real boss was.

He pulled to the side of the Turnpike, and I climbed into the back. I put the bag of sugar "crack" in front of me on the floor, and he pulled out into traffic.

For the next hour, I ate. I stuffed myself. I vacuumed up every morsel of food I'd bought. If it involved opening cellophane wrappers, I did it as quietly as possible, convinced that if I was careful he wouldn't hear, which was ridiculous. But he didn't say a thing.

By the time we arrived in New York City, I was completely "drunk." Peter was a recovering alcoholic. Some people think that all addicts understand each other. It's not true. No matter how much I tried to explain that I binged on food just as he had binged on alcohol, he didn't get it. Or maybe he was in denial too. So far, it hadn't been a problem in our relationship, as I was doing all the things I was supposed to do and was not abusing food. The biggest food problem we'd had was that he strongly believed you shouldn't take food home from a restaurant, and I never wanted to waste any food; I couldn't leave uneaten food on the table any more than I could fly to the moon. So we agreed to disagree, and I got to take my leftovers home.

I had instinctively known from the beginning that Peter not only wouldn't understand about food addiction but also would be judgmental about it. So I just tried to hide it from him. My bingeing episodes were getting closer and closer together, harder to hide, and we'd never spent a long stretch of time together. My attention wasn't on him or what we were doing. It was on food: When was the next meal? Could I get something before that? Could I last until dinner? How could I eat something without him seeing?

Peter was not dumb. He never said anything, but I'm sure he knew something was very wrong and that I was hiding it from him. He also had a black-and-white way of seeing the world. There was a right way and a wrong way to do things, and he knew the right way. It was hard for him to embrace things he didn't understand and be supportive. In my deluded thinking, I thought that by hiding my food addiction from him, I would save myself from his judgments and opinions. I always talked myself into thinking I could get well, and he would never know a thing.

The weekend in New York City was meant to be a birthday present to me from Peter. (We saw the musical *42nd Street*. Many years later, I saw it again, and realized I didn't remember one word or one dance step from the first time. I'd been so drunk on food I'd been incapable of retaining anything.) For me, the weekend is lost. I can't tell you where we stayed, whether it was one night or two nights, or about anything else we did other than seeing *42nd Street*.

For Peter, it was the beginning of the end. He'd had enough of trying to be in relationship with a woman who couldn't show up to be part of the couple but was quick to point out his shortcomings. Another relationship fallen victim to my addiction.

In Princeton, he dropped me off without coming in, and he was gone—back to the Bay Area. I waltzed in to my mother's home with the insane idea that she was lucky that I was willing to come celebrate with her.

For the anniversary party, my mother had filled the house with their friends from the university. My father was now able to sit in a wheelchair for extended periods of time, but he couldn't move himself around, so he just sat and watched. To me, it seemed that many were in total denial of how hard it was to communicate with Daddy. Some people made more of an effort than others. My aunt sometimes came over and sang for him, remembering how much he loved musicals. Others took him for "walks" in his wheelchair. The majority of people were uncomfortable. My father had been a force, a very

popular professor and brilliant academician. It was hard for everyone
to see him in the state he was in. He gave no clues regarding how
much he understood. He pointed his finger to try to make a point,
and when we didn't understand, his whole face fell in defeat.

My relationship with my mother was terrible—toxic and mean
and painful. I still blamed her for everything that was wrong in my
life. I don't know what she thought of me, except that she didn't much
like me.

Every time I returned to the house in Princeton, I did the same
thing: I walked in the front door, went the twenty steps to the kitchen,
and started opening all the cabinets. Nothing ever changed in the
cabinets or in my behavior. I kept looking and searching, hoping for
something new to eat. Time after time. Visit after visit. Each time,
I ended up eating all her nut mix that she kept in the last cabinet I
looked in. Each time, I was unsatisfied. Whatever I was looking for
wasn't there.

My mother didn't much like food. She told me once that she would
just as soon eat cardboard as food. It was all the same to her. As she
got older and there was no one to eat with, she snacked more than ate
meals. She loved her nut mix, but a twelve-ounce jar that I could have
scarfed in one sitting would last one or two months for her.

When I came to Princeton, the refrigerator was usually three-quarters empty. I took it as a sign that my mother didn't love me, as she
never once asked me what I would like when I was visiting, that she
would be sure to have it there for me. In my mind, that meant she
didn't love me.

The living room/dining room, where her guests were gathered,
was arranged like an upside-down L. The kitchen was right off the
dining room, separated by a swinging door. Whoever had helped my
mother prepare for the party had cooked a huge turkey. Everything
was laid out, buffet style, on a table in the dining room. I helped to
make sure people's glasses were topped off. People filled their plates

and socialized in the living room, and I made conversation with the people I knew.

It had been fourteen years since I'd left Princeton for California. My mother was now teaching at Rutgers Medical School, and it had been four years since my father's stroke. I knew enough of the cast to be social . . . until the obsession and cravings descended on me. It seemed the time between these bouts of complete obsession was getting shorter and shorter.

Under the guise of being super helpful and efficient, I carried all the finished plates sitting on various surfaces into the kitchen where I proceeded to finish off all the turkey on the plates. Each time I returned to the kitchen, I tore hunks of turkey off the carcass and stuffed myself. I didn't try to be pretty about it. I just needed to do it fast and before anyone could see me. The kitchen was too close to the party for comfort. I was cutting it close. It would be very easy for someone to walk in on me bingeing. On the one hand, I was terrified of being caught eating. On the other, I wasn't scared enough not to do it. I walked around the house, looking for more plates to bus, and when I couldn't find any more, I sat in the kitchen and finished off all the meat on the carcass.

I didn't have it in me to wait until people had left the party. I couldn't pretend to be interested in anyone or in any more discussions. I was completely hostage to my compulsions. I had no "enough" button; I just binged until the need to keep doing it went away, or until I fell asleep.

The cravings were coming more and more frequently. My disease was in the fast lane. So was the denial.

That night, I lay in bed, terrified. The food was no longer working to numb me. Panic was taking over as awareness came. I couldn't keep my eyes closed. I had lost all ability to control my food intake. I felt wretched from the bingeing. I was stuffed; my stomach was stretched to what seemed like a breaking point. I prayed for sleep to put me out of my misery.

When I couldn't sleep, I called the airlines and reserved a seat on a plane back up to Boston the next day. I was leaving Princeton three days before I was scheduled to. I had to do something, and I didn't know what else to do but that. The meeting in Harvard Square was what I was thinking about.

It was 1:00 a.m., too late to call my sister. I would call her in the morning. I had a plan to wake up the next morning and leave. "You're running away again?" my mother shouted at me as I packed my suit-case. "Once more, you promised to help me with your father. Once more, you're leaving. Why am I not surprised?"

I wanted to yell, "Fuck you!" What I said was, "I have to leave, you don't understand."

"Oh, I understand, alright. You are only thinking of yourself."

I kept my mouth shut.

"Just wait till you have children. I hope they treat you like you treat me."

I left and walked to the bus stop. Her words fell on the mountain of resentments I held inside.

Twice in one week, I was landing at Logan airport. I took a cab to the same motel I had stayed in a week earlier. I found a little convenience store and bought cans of tuna, cans of green beans, and a Danielle Steel paperback. I locked myself in my room, too scared of being out-side any longer on my own. I kept calling my sister until I finally reached her. I stuffed my pride in my pocket and asked her for help.

"I'm back in Boston, Vicki. I walked out on Mommy. I was

bingeing and bingeing and all I could think about was the meeting you took me to last Friday. She's furious, and I'm terrified. Please help me?" I was pleading. I didn't actually know if she would help. She had so many resentments toward me.

"Well, good for you for getting back up here," she said. "Don't think about Mommy right now. I don't think it's a good idea for me to be the one to help you, but I will put you in touch with someone who can."

God bless her.

True to her word, a woman named Joan called me within thirty minutes.

"Hi, Sara. I'm Vicki's friend in the program. Do you have a pencil and paper?"

I opened drawers in the motel room and found paper. I had a pen.

"Write down my address. Tomorrow, take a cab here. I'll leave a key in the planter outside my apartment door. Then I want you to go to the noon meeting. Raise your hand, say you are new, and scared, and could someone stay with you after the meeting. Stay until the five thirty meeting. When you get back in the evening, I'll be home from work, and we can talk."

I'd heard about people reaching out like this in Alcoholics Anonymous but had never experienced it in OA. I felt like a child who was now safe because I had explicit directions I could follow.

"Should I buy food for dinner for you and me?" I asked her.

"Don't worry about that. You just worry about getting here and getting yourself to those meetings."

It felt like a huge relief that she was treating me like the addict than I am. She knew what to do with people just like me. People who were obsessed with food, who binged all the time and couldn't stop. Who could possibly understand but another compulsive eater?

For the next four days, I did precisely as I was told. I met many of the slim, happy people that I'd seen at the meeting the Friday before. They were all patient with me, shared their stories with me, and let me have all the hope I needed. I felt cared about. I felt understood, maybe for the first time in my life. And I felt safe. As long as I hung out with these people, whatever was wrong with me was in remission. I met a wonderful woman named Sarah who told me to call her from California every morning and tell her exactly what food I would be eating that day *before* I ate anything. She gave me a food plan printed on a grey sheet. Then she gave me these guidelines:

1. Buy a scale and a set of measuring cups.

2. Weigh and/or measure every single morsel of food that goes in your mouth.

3. Eat three meals a day with nothing in between but coffee, tea, or diet soda, and, of course, water.

4. Eat only the foods that are written down on the food plan. (Fortunately, they were bountiful.)

5. Eat each meal between three to seven hours after the one before (except breakfast).

6. Read the ingredients on the outside of everything you buy. If sugar is the fourth ingredient or higher, it's too high in sugar content and you're not to eat it.

I was finally admitting to myself that I didn't know anything about caring for myself. This community of fellow food addicts told me I was carbohydrate sensitive, that my body couldn't tolerate sugar, grains, or refined carbohydrates in either liquid or hard form. Putting any of those ingredients in my body would set off the craving.

What made it possible for me to follow these new directions I was receiving was the clarity of the instructions. I was not being told to pull my bootstraps up and eat in moderation. I was not being told to be more disciplined. I was not being told for the thousandth time, "You have such a pretty face, why don't you just try harder."

"Try harder at what?" I always wanted to scream.

Now, with assuredness and confidence, I was being told *exactly* what to do. Now, I had people telling me, "You have a very serious problem. That's the bad news. The good news is that there is a solution. The solution requires that you accept that you have a disease that is similar to alcoholism."

What did that mean?

"It means," they told me, "you have a disease of the mind and the body. It means that you can't use willpower to treat this disease any more than you could treat your own cancer if you had that. YOU NEED HELP. And you can have our help, all you want, any time of the day."

Most people, upon hearing this, breathe a huge sigh of relief. *REALLY? There's hope? You understand?*

"Yes, we understand," people were saying to me. "We promise you do not have to suffer with not knowing why any longer. We'd be lying, however, if we told you this was easy. It is simple, but you can't cut corners as you've done your whole life, hoping to get somewhere faster or trick someone into grading you well. There are no grades; this is not a moral issue. You have a disease, and there are simple, suggested guidelines for recovery."

I told my new friend, Sarah, that I was in. I wanted to do this. I liked her, and I wanted what she had. She was petite, with dark, wavy hair and dancing brown eyes. When she talked to me and told me her story of food addiction, she looked straight at me. She was educated, I could tell by the way she spoke to me. She was absolutely straight with me. She didn't gush and tell me everything would be fine. Neither one of us knew if that was true. She sat there with me in the Cambridge sunshine and said, "This has worked for me, and I hope it works for you."

"I'll do it. I'll call you every day. I'll do whatever you tell me to do." I told her.

And I meant it 100 percent at the time. But this disease is insidious, and it's a disease that insists it's not a disease. It's a disease of amnesia.

I returned to California on September 4, 1983, armed with hope and people's prayers for me. Little did I know that it would take another twenty-two years before I would be convinced that this solution was my *only* hope.

13

A Head Full of Program and a Belly Full of Food

There is a saying in Alcoholics Anonymous: "There is nothing worse than a head full of AA and a belly full of booze." That was my life for the next twenty-two years: knowing that there was a solution out there that arrested food addiction, but unable to let go of my resistance to it.

I knew the Cambridge version of OA worked, because I followed the program for five months. During that time, I lost weight, my head cleared up, and physically I felt great.

In twelve-step rooms, amongst people in recovery, we have sayings that are funny but also pinpoint an obstacle that is universal amongst addicts. We hear these sayings and smile or laugh because we have become honest enough to know that they are 100 percent true.

A man named Jack was walking along the top of a steep cliff one day when he accidentally got too close to the edge and fell. On the way down, he grabbed a branch, which temporarily stopped his fall. He looked down and, to his horror, saw that the canyon fell straight down for more than a thousand feet. He couldn't hang on to the branch forever, and there was

*no way for him to climb up the steep wall of the cliff. So Jack
began yelling for help, hoping that someone passing by would
hear him and lower a rope or something.*

"HELP! HELP! Is anyone up there? HELP!"

*He yelled for a long time, but no one heard him. He was
about to give up when he heard a voice.*

"Jack. Jack. Can you hear me?"

"Yes, yes! I can hear you. I'm down here!"

"I can see you, Jack. Are you all right?"

"Yes, but who are you, and where are you?"

"I am the Lord, Jack. I'm everywhere."

"The Lord? You mean, GOD?"

"That's Me."

*"God, please help me! I promise if, you'll get me down from
here, I'll stop sinning. I'll be a really good person. I'll serve You
for the rest of my life."*

*"Easy on the promises, Jack. Let's get you out of there;
then we can talk. Now, here's what I want you to do. Listen
carefully."*

"I'll do anything, God. Just tell me what to do."

"Okay. Let go of the branch."

"What?"

"I said, let go of the branch. Just trust Me. Let go."

There was a long silence.

Finally, Jack yelled, "IS ANYONE ELSE UP THERE?"

For twenty-two years, that was me. My sister had taken me to a
meeting. What I'd heard in that meeting had resonated for me. As
often happens when we slow down enough to pay attention, I'd heard
information that I knew was the truth for me. And in the five months
I practiced all those suggestions, I flourished.

Then I let the disease in the door, and I binged.

There I was, the solution to my food addiction in hand: a simple plan printed on a plain grey sheet of paper. But it was hard, and I wanted something easier. In spite of knowing in my gut and in my heart that I already had found the answer, I kept yelling in the dark, "Is there another solution out there?"

I refused to let go and trust in the solution.

It's not easy surrendering to a solution that says, "Everything you thought you knew about food, about nutrition, about losing weight, and about your size is wrong." It was next to impossible for me to accept that, although I had read at least one hundred books on nutrition, had gone to graduate school for psychology, and had been seeing therapists for ten years, when it came to the disease of food addiction, none of that was helpful. I believed there was another answer out there and that it was only because I was so defective that I couldn't find it.

It took twenty-two years of banging my head up against brick walls, paying thousands of dollars to a therapist, trying more and more diets and losing the weight, only to gain it all back plus more, to finally accept that, in fact, I was not defective. I had a disease—a disease of being addicted to sugar, grains, and refined carbohydrates—and my insistence on sticking my head in the sand instead of accepting that fact was destroying everything of value in my life.

My home in California was in an area affectionately known as Baja Piedmont or sometimes even the Piedmont Ghetto. The city of Piedmont was like the hole in a doughnut. Completely surrounded by Oakland, it had its own post office, its own little city hall, and people paid very different (higher) taxes. The Piedmont schools were significantly better than those in Oakland, and to many that was worth the higher taxes. Piedmont was home to mansions and society folk from the Blue Book. Everything was beautiful there: gardens were well kept, trees were constantly trimmed, and there were parks within walking distance of most homes.

Then there was where I lived, in a small, concrete, two-bedroom, one-bath house close to the Oakland border. I had one phone, with a cord so long I could carry it to most places in the house. I spent many hours on the phone with Sarah, learning both how to weigh and measure my food and how to survive withdrawal symptoms.

It was difficult for me to believe that I had a disease—that this was an "ism," just like alcoholism. I had been trained so well in the world of dieting, and to believe that anyone could do it if they would just _____ [fill in the blank]. Yet I was experiencing classic withdrawal symptoms. I got horrible headaches. I'd get energy rushes, and Sarah would tell me to wash my floors—that this was a good use of that energy. I would sleep too much or not nearly enough. I'd feel sick when nothing seemed to be wrong with me. Sarah had to remind me over and over that what was happening was normal, and that it would pass.

"God bless your abstinent misery," she'd say to me. "Whatever it is you are feeling, you are abstaining from that poison."

Meanwhile, she taught me to practice all the new things I had to do. I had to learn to shop and to cook and to read the ingredients on the labels of food.

In September, I started two OA meetings similar to the ones I'd attended in Cambridge in the Bay Area. Since the food plan was printed on a grey piece of paper, it somehow seemed very loving that the Cambridge people called the meetings Greysheet meetings. My relationship with Sarah, my sponsor, felt critical to me during this time. I could ask her questions and get concrete rather than theoretical answers—and, if appropriate, she'd share examples of things she'd seen other people do successfully in Cambridge.

At that time, in 1983, Greysheet OA meetings were only on the

East Coast. Most were in Cambridge or Boston. Some new meetings were opening up in New York City. Though OA was founded in Los Angeles and this food plan was the one everyone had used, it had gone out of fashion as nutrition began to dictate the food plans available. I was the first person to bring these meetings back out to the West Coast. The structure was very similar to Alcoholics Anonymous meetings. When necessary, and with permission, we changed the word "alcohol" to "food."

I found a room in a church that wouldn't charge me anything until I had a group and got enough money through member donations. Then we'd be able to pay a small rent.

The church gave me the room on Tuesday evenings and Saturday mornings. I put the day and time in the Bay Area OA meeting list, which was updated every three months, and I waited for people to come.

In the beginning, I sat by myself or a friend came to sit with me. As the days turned into weeks, some people from Cambridge moved out to the Bay Area. They told me that they were so happy and felt safe now that there were these meetings in the Bay Area. Meanwhile, I talked to many of my friends that I had met in Overeaters Anonymous and told them how different the OA/Greysheet program was for someone like me, a hardcore food addict. The Greysheet food plan provided clarity. It had definite guidelines for what we could and couldn't eat, and the amounts to eat at each meal. Like AA, it was black and white. Having a precise structure, I told my friends, had turned out to be an absolute must. The boundaries allowed me safety. Plus, I didn't have to keep falling back on my own faulty thinking. Some of those OA people migrated over to these meetings.

Just two months after we started, we had as many as ten to twelve people coming to the meetings. It was starting to feel easier for me. I had stuck little yellow pieces of paper all over my kitchen to remind me of the most important parts of the program: "Don't eat no matter what;" "Three meals a day, nothing in between." I couldn't imagine that anything could happen to make me not want to continue with this amazing food plan and program, to give up feeling the way I felt.

At that time, no one was encouraging us to do the rest of the twelve steps. It seemed hard enough doing Step One: *admit we were powerless over food—that our lives had become unmanageable.* At that point, I was probably accepting Step One about 50 percent of the time. I didn't like the word "powerless." As long as it was easy to eat my three meals a day, I didn't really think about the meaning and the principle of Step One: surrender. I certainly had no respect for the notion of a disease. I still thought I could control everything.

I'd been raised during the Women's Movement of the 1970s, a time when women were taking back their power. I had written my master's thesis on crisis counseling programs that a women's cooperative in Berkeley was gifting to women who were working with populations in crisis. I wanted to feel that I had some control over my life. I hated feeling vulnerable and helpless, and when it came to food, I felt those emotions all the time. I didn't understand that Step One only referred to me being powerless when it came to *food.* I thought that if I accepted Step One, I was giving up all power and all control over my entire life.

I also had no comprehension of what it meant that my life might be unmanageable. I knew from experience that when I was under the influence of sugar and carbs, I could barely get out of bed. I couldn't manage a day, much less my life. I called it being depressed. I had bought into being a victim. I blamed most everyone else for the things that weren't working in my life, especially my family. I could not wrap my brain cells around the idea that getting my food under control would have huge repercussions on how I looked at the world in general. Telling me that my life was unmanageable and that I was powerless was the equivalent of telling me I had no control and was a weak person. I could admit that I was severely depressed, but no one else was allowed to put labels on what I was feeling.

An example: My office in Oakland was in a beautiful old Victorian home that my supervisor had bought years before. She was renting me one of the rooms for a very fair price. I had a fair number of clients. The driveway was to the left of the building and had an uphill slant as it made its way toward the back. One day, after having binged all morning on granola that led to cookies that led to anything else I could find in my home, I got myself in my car and to my office. My office was close to the front door, so when someone knocked, about fifteen minutes into my first session of the day, I heard it. I excused myself and went to open the door, and standing there was my neighbor from the bagel shop next door.

"Sorry to bother you, Sara, but your car is sitting in the middle of Piedmont Avenue."

What? I stepped out of the door and onto the first step, where I could see the street. Sure enough, there was my four-door sedan, right in the middle of Piedmont Avenue, obstructing traffic. Cars were slowing down to circle around it. It was a miracle that no one had run into it.

I told my client I would be right back and got my keys. As I opened the door to the car, I wished the earth would open up and swallow me whole. No one was screaming at me as they passed. No one yelled a curse word or called me a stupid bitch. I was the only one berating myself and drowning in shame and humiliation. No one but me knew what I'd done—that I'd failed to put the emergency brake on because I was too spaced out on food. To me, it seemed that there was a glaring neon sign over my head that said: FOOD ADDICT—DANGER.

When I binged after five months of following the Greysheet food plan, it was a doozy. Not just a little binge but an all-nighter. Part of my sick thinking told me that if something was a health food, or from the health food aisle, then it wasn't problematic. So, although nuts were definitely not on the food plan, they called out to me when I was in the supermarket. I was drawn to the huge bins that looked like wine barrels and held nuts, candy-covered pretzels, and granola, all under signs that said "Eat healthy."

It had been my practice before starting the Greysheet plan to stick my hand in those bins, grab as much as I could, and eat as I walked through the market. My doozy binge started that way. I walked into my local Safeway, stuck my hand in a bin, and wolfed down the first bite, and as the sugar went into my body, my disease was activated. The cravings began immediately, and I kept returning to the bins, stealing more and more nuts and sugar-coated pretzels. Finally, I broke down and bought a couple of large bags of "healthy snacks." Within thirty minutes, I went from "We don't eat no matter what" in between meals to rationalizing that I wasn't sure which product would satisfy me, and it was therefore necessary to buy it all.

In spite of trying as hard as I could, I still wasn't able to trigger vomiting by putting my finger down my throat. I was not bulimic.

After not having had sugar, grains, and carbohydrates for five months, I couldn't get enough. I went back to the grocery store later that evening and filled up on cookies, brownies, and ice cream—all the usual suspects that I had binged on my entire life.

Life and its many problems had kept happening between my meals. I hadn't grasped the concept of "No Matter What" that had so inspired me at my first meeting in Cambridge. I lied to my fellow recovering food addicts. I said I was still abstaining. I shared my story at a meeting and practically fell asleep in a drunken stupor while I was talking. Someone had to interrupt me after I had talked for almost forty-five minutes. I was so ashamed, I disappeared from the meetings. I stopped calling Sarah. I stuck my head in the sand and drowned myself in food and self-pity. Why me? Why couldn't I get this thing called abstinence? Why did it seem that everyone but me was successful at it?

I wouldn't go back to another OA/Greysheet meeting for fourteen years. I did periodically attend regular OA meetings for months at a time, only to disappear and then return again months and months later.

In the 1980s, Piedmont Avenue was just becoming the very upscale place it was later well known for. Across the street and down a block from my office was one of the most popular ice cream parlors in the Bay Area: Fenton's. When a craving hit and I needed to eat, all I wanted to do was go straight to Fenton's and scarf down as much ice cream as I could. Yet I continued to believe that "this time it would be different"—that I could control my intake.

At least once a month, during a break between clients, I would leave my office and walk down the left-hand side of the street, stopping at every food shop along the way—Bagel Heaven, CVS for packages of sugar-free candy, the small gas station across from the Piedmont Theatre for low-calorie chocolate chip cookies. My hope and intention was that by the time I got to Fenton's, I would be too full to buy ice cream. I'd cross the street and walk into Piedmont Grocery. I'd buy tons of healthy snacks, like carrots, telling myself if

I filled up on carrots I wouldn't be able to consume so much sugar. I'd eat until my stomach was stretched to bursting.

This was not a new phenomenon. I was very familiar with it. There were times I thought my stomach was so full my skin would burst open. It was such a frightening feeling, but not frightening enough to stop the binge. I kept eating.

By the time I got to Fenton's, I'd be so sick I could barely stand up. I'd still buy the ice cream and eat it. I couldn't taste it. I wanted to lie down somewhere. It was all I could do to get back to my office and sit down. For the millionth time, I'd reprimand myself for not just going to Fenton's first. If I was going to binge, why not go for the best? But that never happened. It didn't happen because I *always* thought, *This time it will be different.* This time I'd be able to manage the binge and fill up on low-calorie foods, be able to skip the high-calorie stuff and not gain weight. This time, I'd somehow manage to cheat the monster that lived inside of me.

I love live theater. Since I couldn't afford tickets, I became a volunteer usher over multiple seasons in the late 1980s. When plays and musicals came to San Francisco, people like me were called up and asked if we'd help out. I ushered for some of the best shows that came through San Francisco, but I'd only remember about a quarter of them.

For the show *CATS*, I took BART over to the city and got there early, as required. I was dressed in my uniform: a white blouse and black pants.

I was considered a good usher, as I always smiled and treated the patrons as if they were guests in my home. I usually got the orchestra floor.

At this particular matinee, while escorting patrons to their seats, I was obsessing about the food at the bar located in the front entryway of the theater. Patrons had to pass it to find the door that would tell them which side of the stage they would be sitting on. I told myself I could wait it out. *Just finish ushering, then find a seat as far away from the doors to the lobby and food as possible.* But rational thinking was Chinese to me.

I sat down. Within fifteen minutes, I walked up the aisle closest to the wall, exited, and bought a box of candy. *It's ok, Sara,* I told myself. *Just this one time.* I'd put it in my purse. I found my way back to my seat, treading lightly so as not to disturb anyone.

I finished the box in less than five minutes. Out I went again. I took that trip up the aisle and out to the bar, bought another expensive box of candy, walked down the aisle, and got back in my seat. I must have done this six or seven times. I wonder what the bartender must have been thinking. Or if he even cared.

I have no memory of seeing *CATS* that day. In fact, I didn't see it. I was there in the theater, I was in full view of the stage, but all my attention was focused on feeding the voracious beast within. I knew better. I was armed with the knowledge of what happened to me when I ate sugar. Yet I had no power to stop the binge. I was completely hostage to the cravings, and all my knowledge, all my therapy, all my book reading was useless. I felt stupid, ashamed, completely crazy, and very, very lonely.

Even though I'd stopped going to the Greysheet meetings, I was still going to OA meetings and still trying to work the steps, even though I wasn't practicing anything that I read. The second step of the twelve steps of recovery reads, "Came to believe that a power greater than ourselves could restore us to sanity."

Restoring myself to sanity implied that I was insane. That offended me to no end. Of course, I was sane. I had graduated college. I had gone to graduate school, studied for and passed my licensure exam. I was building a successful private practice in the Bay Area. I was in therapy. How could anyone possibly suggest that I was insane?

Well, the answer was simple, but I didn't like it so I refused to listen. Again, I took the narrow interpretation and applied it to my whole life, looking to be offended. Because when it came to sugar, carbohydrates, and grains, *I acted insanely.* I refused with every fiber of my being to see the obvious—that every time I put a morsel of those ingredients into my body, it set off the phenomenon of craving. Over and over and over it happened. I was Jekyll and Hyde, but Hyde had all the power. No matter how many times I told myself that the next time it would be different, it was never different. Never.

If you're not a food addict, you are probably saying, "Wait a minute, Sara, you just told me that the same thing happens 100 percent of the time—not just for a couple of months but for your entire life! You must be insane to think it would ever be different."

Yes, exactly.

14

Under the Influence

By the late '80s, I was becoming a successful therapist. The pain of my youth and the beginnings of understanding the twelve-step programs gave me a lot of compassion for others. When someone sat in my office, they trusted me enough to be vulnerable and tell me their stories, and each time that happened, I found myself liking that person a lot. I think they knew that, and it made them open up even more.

I was also a great actress. It didn't matter if I was dying inside; I would sit down, smile, put on my therapist's hat, and manage to temporarily file away how sick I was, how bloated I was, how crazy I was acting. I could be present for others.

But the bingeing and iron will/white-knuckling attempts to manage my food intake were taking a huge toll on my health. I was tired almost all the time. I had to exert tremendous willpower just to show up at my office every day. Once there, though, I didn't have to think about myself. I didn't realize it at the time but I was learning a great truth: When I was helping other people, I didn't think about myself at all—and that gave me energy. It gave me a reprieve from the self-centered, obsessive thinking.

Outside my office, though, I was dragging. All I could think about was myself and how miserable I was. I made excuses to not go to parties or events with my friends. I was losing a social life. It would be more truthful to say the addiction was robbing me of a social life— as it had robbed me of learning how to be in relationship; as it had robbed me of the tools required to be a grown-up.

In 1987, I hit upon the crazy idea that I needed to change something big. I looked around me and saw that in many other professions, people took sabbaticals. I convinced myself that that was exactly what I needed: time away from psychology to rest and revive. Never mind that the best me showed up in my office. Never mind that the structure of showing up to work every day was giving me a reason to get out of bed in the morning. I made up my mind that a sabbatical was what was best, and that was that.

It took me a number of months to act on this new plan, because I was determined to make sure that all my clients had another therapist to go to that they would like before I stopped working. I didn't leave a single person hanging. I cared for my clients in a way that was completely inaccessible to me when it came to caring for myself.

One of the first things I did after beginning my sabbatical was take a hiking trip with a friend, Alex, her father, and some of their family friends.

I had met Alex in one of the classes I had taken with my supervisor. She was beautiful; I thought she looked like Jackie Kennedy. She was tall, with dark brown hair and a big smile that always felt welcoming. As we'd gotten to be better friends, she'd asked me about Overeaters Anonymous. I couldn't imagine why she wanted the information—in my mind, all compulsive eaters were fat—until she confessed that she binged and purged. Her weight never changed much, but the craziness that went on between her ears was something I recognized. She thought just as I did. Twenty-four hours a day, she thought about food—what she was going to eat, what she was not going to eat, how ugly she was. I looked at her, my beautiful friend, and saw someone who really believed she was ugly. I could see the insanity in her, but I couldn't see it in myself.

Alex had started attending OA meetings with me, and having that intimate secret between us had cemented our friendship. We both understood that we were struggling with something very serious. I felt safe around her. So, when she'd invited me to join the hiking group, I'd jumped at the opportunity. Not only was it a great way to start my sabbatical but I would also be with someone who I could talk to if I started feeling crazy around the food.

We drove southeast from the Bay Area to a spot below Mt. Whitney in the Sequoia & Kings Canyon National Parks. I suppose my expectation was to return to the wonderful feelings of being at summer camp in Vermont. I wanted to surround myself with the kind of natural beauty I'd been in when I had liked myself in the past. But I was out of shape, and my body was exhausted and sick from so much bingeing, so much sugar and not enough good food. Still, I told myself it would be okay, that I loved hiking. I wanted to believe that something that had made me feel good in the past would work again.

The Sara that was a summer camp counselor would have prepared for the trip by taking long walks wearing a backpack with heavy books in it. The Sara that was losing the battle and becoming a full-time "drunk" on food didn't even try to prepare. That Sara convinced herself that some magic would happen and her forty-year-old body wouldn't betray her, even though she'd been treating that body like a garbage can.

The beginning of the hike was not difficult. With packs on our backs, our little party of six hikers slowly ascended to the bottom of Mount Whitney. Everyone was forty or older, so we didn't try to push ourselves. We hiked about five hours a day, then made our camp in the late afternoon.

I wasn't following a food plan. I was going through a phase where I had convinced myself that all the dieting and restrictions were making everything worse—that I should just try to eat "normally." I had never eaten normally in my life, but at forty years old, sick and exhausted from self-destruction, I insanely thought it was as good a time as any to try. Normal eaters don't feel tremendous shame if they eat trail mix or chocolate chip cookies; why couldn't I be one of those people?

I ate the trail mix with raisins and M&Ms. No sooner did I have sugar in my body than I was planning how to get more without anyone else noticing. I had convinced myself I would be safe on this trip because Alex was there. But when I wanted to eat trail mix, my shame forced me to hide my bingeing even from her. I couldn't ask for help because I would have to admit I was bingeing and needed help. My disease didn't want to stop eating. Dishonesty with myself and others was now a way of life for me.

On the fourth day of backpacking, we decided to spend the entire day in one place—to take a rest or do some looking around without our packs. A couple of us left our packs at the campsite and started climbing up rocks—something I had always loved—getting as high on the eastern slope of Mt. Whitney as we could possibly go. But these weren't the small Vermont mountains that people on the West Coast thought of as big hills. Mount Whitney is a true mountain. At 14,505 feet, it is the tallest mountain in California and the highest summit in the contiguous United States. We were far above the tree line. By the time we crested one of the lower peaks, there was nothing but huge rocks and boulders. I was not in shape to climb this kind of mountain, even if we weren't going to the top.

On my way down, I stepped from one large rock to the one below and heard something in my knee make an awful sound.

By the next morning, my knee had doubled in size. I was limping badly, and I felt a complete fool. After a short conference, it was decided that someone else needed to carry my pack as well as their own. Shame overwhelmed me. I kept apologizing. No one was upset with me for what had happened, but I knew I had brought this on myself by abusing my body, by not feeding it correctly. I wasn't even drinking water. I far preferred Diet Coke. Familiar refrains rang in my head: *Why can't I lose weight? Why can't I get abstinent with OA or that Greysheet plan? You are so stupid! Now you've screwed up again.*

When I got back to Oakland and Kaiser Permanente, I learned that I had re-torn cartilage that I had torn years before in a skiing accident. There wasn't much I could do but keep it bandaged and not walk on it.

Be careful what you ask for. I'd said I wanted rest, and now I was being forced into it.

The year of my sabbatical is a hazy time. I binged through most of it. I was drunk on sugar and carbohydrates and experiencing the same memory problems alcoholics have. I had stopped drinking completely, so there was no doubt what was making me "drunk."

I was in bed or on the couch, reading for the first several months. When my knee had healed, I was too scared to move very far from home. There, I could hide and isolate.

Out of desperation, I started seeing clients again before my nine months were up. Some tiny, sane voice in me knew that structure was my salvation, not the cause of my self-destruction. I had to put some meaning back into my life, or the constant dwelling on myself and what was wrong with me would probably lead to something dangerous, like total isolation from the world.

Some of my clients were very happy to return to me. Others had bonded to their new therapists. The little work I did do helped. I felt better. But it was a tiny Band-Aid for the wound I was suffering from. The idea that an addict could manage non-structured time was total insanity. Yet I was still offended by that word.

Why couldn't I accept what was right in front of my eyes? "Why" was now an internal whip that I was using to beat myself up with on a daily basis. I wasn't asking a question; I was making a statement. I was wallowing in self-pity.

What I wanted more than anything else in the world back then was to be thin and to eat whatever I wanted whenever I wanted. That was about as possible as walking on air. It never once occurred to me that thin people didn't eat the way I fantasized about eating. Eating whatever one wants whenever one wants is not normal—and it was what I was already doing. Consequently, I was yo-yoing between fat and slightly heavy.

I was falling deeper and deeper into depression, hopelessness, and self-pity. I had three choices in front of me: stop bingeing, which meant total acceptance of my food addiction and going back to the Greysheet recovery program; go completely insane; or, probably, die. Only an addict would ponder over those options.

15

Fire

I was back at work. I was attending both OA and AA meetings. If I had any success with my weight, it was because I was dieting. And I was desperate to find a man. I was convinced that if I could just find someone to love me, my problems would all be solved. I had a very low bar. If someone seemed to like me, that was all I needed to know about him. I was forty-three years old, and I had had only one long relationship. It had worked as long as it had because we'd been good friends before we fell in love. I had no idea how to have a loving relationship and yet, ironically, because I was a therapist, I thought I was an expert on the subject. The inability to play well with others is one of the main characteristics of the addict. I wanted to be loved so badly. I didn't love myself, so I wanted someone else to do it for me.

At my AA meetings, I met and socialized with a lot of recovering alcoholic men. I used AA as a social club. I dated and slept with one guy after another. They call it serial monogamy. I would flirt and if he flirted back, I fell in love, ecstatic that someone liked me.

When I was in lust or "in love," I wasn't hungry. I could eat somewhat like I thought a normal person ate. But I was aware every minute of the day that I wasn't bingeing, and as the weight came off, I would strut around like a peacock, looking in every mirror, in every window, as if I had done something extraordinary.

179

During this time, I went on a couple of dates with a guy named Joe. He was nice—a bit shy, quite intelligent, and he treated me like I was made of thin glass. One night, we went to an AA dance. (In the '80s, social get-togethers, like dances, were a regular weekly event for AA members.) Joe and I danced and talked. Then I saw a man named Steven that I'd run into a lot at meetings. He asked me to dance. He was British, very sexy, and a good dancer, and I was very attracted to him. I went back and forth between the two men, dancing first with one and then the other. Finally, I couldn't stand it. I asked Joe to take me home. As soon as he drove away, I jumped in my car and drove back to the dance so I could be with Steven. I didn't think about who would see me and perhaps tell Joe that I had come back. I didn't think about whether it would cause him any hurt. I just wanted what I wanted.

My relationship with Steven lasted a couple of months and ended on a sour note. Why? I don't really remember. But as with so many of my "relationships," he probably hurt my feelings and, feeling insulted and abused, I argued with him until I drove him away. When that happened, once again, I felt victimized, a position that was very familiar. Things were never my fault.

With Steven, with Joe, the chase was over after the first or second time of sleeping together. Then the fog lifted. From having no expectations or requirements, I'd become critical and resentful if the guy wasn't the perfect mate.

Let me be clear: These were nice enough people. But they were as emotionally arrested as I was. Being in AA was giving them a chance to grow up. Not me. I wasn't there to grow or work hard, even though I was telling myself that was the reason I went to meetings. Looking back, it was obvious that I was there to be social. It's not necessarily a bad thing to want to belong to a group and be social, but I was lying to myself. I was telling myself I was there for one reason when in fact I stayed for a completely different one. I just wanted that high feeling of flirting and chasing and being chased and sought after. Falling in love was just another drug.

Once, at a party, after listening to me complain about someone I was dating, a friend looked at me and said, "Sara, like attracts like."

I didn't talk to that friend again for a long time. I hated him. I was insulted.

In 1991, my father, who had now lived for twelve years as a stroke patient, died. His birthday was April 11. That day, I called my mother to have her wish him a happy birthday from me, and she told me he'd had another small stroke. She didn't say anything more.

That afternoon, as I was getting a massage, I suddenly got a strong feeling that there was much more my mother wasn't telling me.

"Celeste," I said, "can we stop? And can I borrow your phone? My dad had another stroke. I think I need to call my mother."

"Of course, Sara," she said kindly. "I'll just wait outside the door until you are finished."

I dialed, and when my mother picked up, I said, "Mom, I know we just talked earlier, but you aren't telling me everything."

There was a moment of silence.

Then: "The stroke was small, Sara, but it's cut off his ability to swallow. He needs a tube in his stomach in order to be fed."

I was trying to picture this and didn't like what I was visualizing.

"I'm going to come back there to see you guys. Would that be okay?"

"That's wonderful," she said. "I do need you."

Really? My mother needed me? I'd been nine years old the last time I had heard her say something of that kind. I had come home from school with a piece of art that I had created in art class: a bowl with an apple, orange, and banana in it. My mother had taken one look at it and gazed at me with wonder in her eyes. "This is wonder-ful, Sara," she'd said. "I'm putting it on a small table where everyone can see it."

That day, I'd felt warm and happy all over. I had the same feeling hearing her say that she needed me now.

"I'm calling the airlines now." I hung up.

My mother had sold the house in Princeton, and she and my father had moved into a Continuing Care Retirement Community called Pennswood Village in Lower Bucks County, Pennsylvania. Daddy had a private room in the Skilled Nursing wing, the third level of care in CCRCs.

When I arrived, I went straight to his room. It was hard to look at him. He was grey. His skin seemed grey, his hair was grey. He was a tiny lump in his twin-size bed. He was asleep and a nurse was with him. He had an IV line inserted in his left arm, just above his wrist, and a gastric tube (G-tube) inserted into his stomach. I watched as the nurse attempted to put back the IV line that kept falling out of his arm. No sooner did she have the needle in than it fell out again. The G-tube was not attached to anything and had a clamp at the end of it.

"That is how we are feeding him," the nurse told me. "We'll attach another tube with nutrition in it later."

"Why are we doing this?" I asked. "It seems cruel." It looked to me like his body was rejecting any attempts to help him stay alive.

"Your mother wants it," she said.

"If my mother agrees, would it be possible to meet with you, the doctor, my mother, and me?" I asked her.

"I don't see why not. The doctor will be here in the morning, and we can set it up then."

When I told my mother about it, she surprised me by being

agreeable to it. I realized that this woman who was intimidatingly bossy and made decisions for everyone else was incapable of dealing with this huge upset. She was scheduled to have back surgery two days after I arrived. It didn't occur to her to reschedule. She couldn't deal with what was right in front of her. If I'd wondered how I'd learned to stick my head in the sand, I was now witnessing my role model in action.

The next morning, we met with the doctor and my dad's nurse, the one I'd spoken to the day before, in a small, sparsely decorated conference room. My mother and the doctor sat opposite each other at a large oval table which filled up the entire room. I sat on my mother's left looking at the nurse across from me.

I looked at the doctor. "I just arrived yesterday and need an update on my father."

"It is bad," he told me. "He can only live with the aid of tubes to feed him and injections of blood on regular intervals."

"What would happen if we took all the lines out of him?" Just uttering the words made me feel like a murderer, but I knew my father would not want to be kept alive in this way.

"He would gradually shut down. He'd probably get pneumonia. We would monitor him and give him morphine to make sure he was in no pain."

I felt completely raw and vulnerable proposing this solution. "Is it something that is alright to do? I mean, wouldn't we be killing him?"

The doctor was kind. "No, we would be leaving it all to the natural course of things."

I looked at my mother.

"You decide," she said. "I can't."

This was not a difficult decision. I had lost my father twelve years earlier. I had never understood until that moment why she hadn't let him go when he was in the coma after his first stroke. Knowing the man my father had been, he wouldn't have wanted to live this way. To keep him alive with tubes coming out of him as his only lifeline seemed like the definition of abuse and cruelty.

So we made the decision to let him go. The doctor removed all the lines and tubes and left it up to a higher power as to how long my father would live.

My mother got her back surgery, and I spent the days while she was in the hospital with my father, feeding him popsicles—the only thing that would slip down his throat. The stroke had cut off all the muscles we use to swallow. The one thing I could give him were the popsicles that melted in his mouth, the liquid sliding down his throat without his aid. Maybe I did this for me, but Daddy had always liked sweet things, so I felt at least I was giving him something he would enjoy. As each day passed and death seemed imminent, however, I got the feeling he was trying to please me.

After three days, I went to pick my mother up at the Hospital of the University of Pennsylvania. She was asleep when I walked into her recovery room, and her arms were lying by her side on top of her blanket. I picked up her left hand and stroked the skin. It was incredibly soft and delicate, like a baby's but thinner. Two words, soft and delicate, that I would never have used to describe my mother. Holding her hand, I felt that longing to be wrapped in her arms, something she'd so seldom done.

She woke up, took back her hand, and things began moving quickly. She was packed up, brought a wheelchair, and loaded into the car in quick succession. And back to her apartment at Pennswood we went.

My mother spent the rest of Daddy's last week in bed, recovering. I spent it by his side trying to practice all the "wonderful" things I had learned in death and dying groups. I found that talking about doing the things I was practicing was completely different than actually doing them. I had to screw up all the courage I had just to ask him, a dying man, if he and I were "clean," meaning no lingering upsets or resentments. He nodded his head: *Yes, we're good.* I asked the nurses for a tape recorder and had soft music playing most of the time. I held his hand and assured him that we were all going to be okay. It was probably one of the most intimate times I'd ever had with him, and I found it very difficult.

The nurses were so encouraging. They were impressed with me, which gave me more courage. My sister, who was now teaching at the University of Michigan, had not yet appeared. I still don't know if she fully comprehended that Daddy was dying. For my part, I was glad to have him to myself. There were no family eyes watching while I bumbled through my good-bye.

Finally, one of the nurses came to me and said, "I don't think your father is going to let go as long as you are here. You might think about leaving and going back to your home."

What she was saying made sense to me. I made reservations to fly back to California that Sunday morning. Vicki arrived a little later that day and got to say good-bye. Daddy died late that afternoon.

My mother had given me adult responsibility for the first time in my life, and I felt I'd risen to the challenge. The hunger in me disappeared during that short time. I didn't binge once while I was there. In many ways, I felt like an imposter. I was being treated as an adult, and I was acting as an adult. I was so used to my mother treating me as an immature child that I feared the rug would be pulled out from under me. I wanted to relish every moment; I wanted to be present for my father. But underneath was a layer of fear telling me this wasn't reality—that I was soon going to be exposed.

In May, six weeks after my father's death, my mother was back in charge. I flew to Princeton for the memorial service she organized. In my father's memory and his honor, Princeton University, where he had taught for sixteen years, gave the family the theater of the Woodrow Wilson School to hold the service in.

At the memorial, the room was packed. Even twelve years after his stroke, past students, other professors, and the community in Princeton had enormous affection for my father. There were prepared speeches, and then people were invited to share. I couldn't get up and talk—I just couldn't do it. I watched as my articulate sister stood and shared a story I'd never heard.

Vicki related that once, during her teens, she was still awake when my father returned home late from a quick trip up to Manhattan. He came into her room and handed her thirty or forty dollars. He told her that he had intended to buy shoes with built-up heels in them so that he would be taller than my mother, but by the time he got to the shoe store, he had changed his mind. He told her that he realized he was fine the way he was, the same height as my mother. He told Vicki to take the money and buy herself something nice.

I cried. I missed my father. In the years to come, after I truly committed to recovery from my addictions, I would think about my father and wonder, *Would he like me?* I know he would always love me—but would he like me?

In October of that same year, my home in Oakland burned down in a firestorm that consumed 3,100 homes. It was the worst urban fire in California's history at the time (though it would later be surpassed in 2017 and again in 2018). The new Oakland fire chief was three weeks into his job and had no experience with this kind of fire. Many mistakes were made. Twenty-five lives were lost. Close to 7,000 of us were left homeless and traumatized.

I lost most everything I owned in the fire. I was home that day and had only one big choice to make: I looked at all my journals that I had been keeping in some form or another for many years and decided not to save them. I would let them burn, crossing my fingers that my miserable history would burn away with them. I thought I was being so Zen, practicing non-attachment. It would only be later, in the writing of this memoir, that I'd be sad not to be able to read about the things I wouldn't remember.

The fire was a huge turning point in my life. For many years afterward, I would refer to my life as BF, Before the Fire, and AF, After the Fire.

The fire actually started on a Saturday afternoon on the Orinda side of the Oakland hills. Someone dropped a lit cigarette in the hot, windy October weather and a small grass fire started. The Orinda Fire Department put it out.

The rule of thumb is that a fire space is monitored for twenty-four hours before being given the "all clear" by a fire department. I was told that the night crew left before assuring themselves that the next crew had arrived. The next crew never arrived—and meanwhile, the weather was a perfect storm. It was hot, the barometer had dropped low, and the winds were gusting up to forty-five miles an hour. A little spark ignited and within minutes the fire was racing up the hills and over into Oakland, where it immediately consumed the Parkland Apartments, the first residences to burn.

My latest boyfriend, M, had spent the night, and we were puttering around when the phone rang. A friend, who was having brunch down at Jack London Square in the flats of Oakland, was calling to ask if I was alright. I had no idea what she meant.

"Sara, we can see flames in the hills and the sky is full of smoke. Isn't it near you?"

Looking out my window, I said, "I don't see anything. I'll get M to investigate."

As soon as we hung up, M climbed up behind my home to a fire trail. From there you could see north across Highway 24 and quite a ways east, all the way to the tunnel going to Orinda. If you walked along the trail far enough, you could also see Lake Temescal, which was about a half-mile west of me.

When M came back, he told me that the fire was on the other side of the freeway and I should come up and see it. I got dressed and the two of us hiked back up to the trail. I was the only woman there amongst nine or ten men. I saw immediately that it was serious. I walked west to look at Lake Temescal—and I looked down on a ring of fire. The fire had completely surrounded the lake and was taking down larger trees and bushes, leaving a very unfamiliar landscape in its wake.

I hurried back to M and the other men. "Lake Temescal is surrounded by flames," I told them. "I can barely see it. The winds always shift south around 1:00 p.m. I think we should go down and pack up our houses."

"Sara, you're overreacting," M said.

"I am not. I'm certain about the winds. I'm going down to the house."

I stomped down the hill, seething with resentment. I hated M. Why couldn't he agree with me? When I got to the house, I banged around without a focus of what to do. I was burning up with anger, but I knew I had to pack up the car. I had two cats and found one, Rosie. I got her into the backseat. She hated cars so much that every time I opened the car door, she jumped out and ran, and I wasted precious time going after her. I couldn't find my other cat, which only added to my angst.

I put laundry in the car. I grabbed my brand-new skis and some expensive jewelry that I had inherited from my grandmother. I also grabbed cheap stuff. I was numb and angry, muttering to myself. M was still up on the fire trail. I decided I would leave at a certain time, with or without M.

As I was getting ready to drive away, a friend from next door said, "Did you grab photos?"

No, I didn't. It hadn't even occurred to me. I went back into the house and grabbed photo albums without really looking to see what was in them.

I saw M. He was grinning as he approached the car. "I'm leaving now." I told him. "Are you coming?" I didn't care if he was or wasn't. "You seem to be enjoying the fire so stay. I don't care."

He got in the car.

I was in the driver's seat but driving erratically. I was crying and pissed off at the same time. Finally, I pulled over and let him drive. We joined a long line of cars attempting to evacuate. At one point the police turned us around when the fire jumped onto the street we were attempting to evacuate onto. The long, snaking lineup of cars all changed directions; we went into Montclair and over into Piedmont, and then to separate destinations.

M, Rosie, and I went to M's apartment in Berkeley. We unpacked the car and put everything in his garage, and then he mixed me a rum and Coke.

I hadn't had alcohol in more than ten years, and M knew it. We just didn't talk about it much; he had never been curious about AA, and I wasn't going to many meetings, so there really was no reason for him to want to know more as he wasn't alcoholic. He had never put a drink in front of me before. But just like that, it seemed like a very good idea to have a drink. So, I drank it.

I was displaced. I hated my boyfriend, but here I was at his apartment. I couldn't find one of my cats and was still burning up with resentment. I poured myself a second rum and Coke.

"I'm going back up to the Claremont Hotel," M told me. "They need volunteers."

He really was enjoying the fire, it wasn't just my imagination. "You're leaving?" I sputtered.

"They need help. I'll be back."

Fuck you and the horse you rode in on.

I hated him even more. Crazy, insane Sara was having nothing but horrible thoughts about him anyway, but the idea that he wouldn't stay and give me comfort made me even more nuts. I made another rum and Coke. He left, and I turned on the TV and watched Oakland burn. Then I stepped out on his huge terrace and saw almost the same thing unfolding right before my eyes. It was unreal.

M lived in the flats of Berkeley. I was surrounded by darkness. The red-orange glow of the fire burned all along the horizon. Its long, frisky fingers reached up to the sky. I felt as if I had walked through the gates of hell.

I had always been mesmerized by fire—from small-scale fires in my fireplace to the giant bonfires we'd had yearly on the Fourth of July in Vermont. This was beautiful in its awesome horror. My head was telling me that nothing in the path of that fire was safe. Yet it sparkled and spun and jumped and danced as if it were performing a ballet.

I deserved another rum and Coke.

The next morning, I insisted we go back up to see if the house had burned. There were police blockades everywhere, but I found a back way to a road above my house. We parked and walked down Broadway Terrace. We were the only humans around.

The first sight I had of my land was just puffs of smoke. The ground was black and grey and rust-colored, and it looked like a bomb had been dropped on it. I began to cry. We walked to where the house had been. Nothing but a huge emptiness. The pine trees were all down and many still glowed red. Walking up to what had been the front door, nails lay as if placed one after the other all the way up the stairs, perfectly aligned. (The difference between a regular fire and a firestorm is the way a house burns. This fire had flames that jumped from roof to roof, set everything aflame at 2,000-degree heat, yet some things on the ground didn't burn at all.)

I walked to where a bookcase should have been. The journals I had chosen not to take with me sat there in perfect shape. They'd all had colorful covers; now, there was nothing but grey. But the ash had maintained the shape of the many journals lying side by side. When I touched them with my index finger, they all crumbled into a hill of ashes.

My dishwasher lay on its back, a big rusty box. I opened it and saw dishes in it that looked like they needed to be washed but otherwise were just fine. The heat of the fire hadn't destroyed these few everyday items. Blobs of melted silver lay all over the place, the remnants of my mother's silver that she had given me. Little bottles of I-didn't-know-what—I had no idea what had been in them—lay on the ground only slightly worn but looking like the expensive bottles often found in antique stores. At the bottom of my stairs, my bicycle and an antique wooden milk-crate sat untouched by the fire.

I stood at the top of my property, where the house had been. I could see quite a lot of the neighborhood. All around me was soot, little fires still burning, brick chimneys standing at attention, and stone steps leading to nowhere. The surprise was that there were two houses still standing in that vast moonscape. Both were new and I learned later that they had new city-coded roofs. It reminded me of the story of the plague passing over Jewish houses at the first Passover.

I called for my cat with no hope of ever seeing him. After about thirty minutes on the property, though, I heard a little meow. From

out of nowhere came my Dave Stewart, named after the Oakland
A's baseball pitcher. He was covered in dirt and fire retardant that
had been dumped from helicopters. He must have gone deep into a
sewage tunnel. I picked him up and was crying again.

I would later understand that I was totally numb, completely in
a state of shock. I actually went to work the day after the fire. Every
client wanted to talk about it and asked how I was. I realized right
away that I couldn't work, couldn't accept money and talk about
myself. I took the next two weeks off.

In the following days, I connected with a representative of my
insurance company. I was given five thousand dollars to buy clothes
and necessities. I bought a cell phone. It was about a foot long, two
inches thick, and cumbersome, but all I needed was to be able to call
in to my voice mail.

Everyone was looking for homes to rent. I found one in Montclair
that was five minutes from the home that was no more. I was twen-
ty-eighth in line for renting it. I called my nice insurance representative and asked if it was possible to pay an entire year's rent all at once.
He said yes, it was. Fortunately for me, the landlord needed money,
and when I made that offer I went to the top of the list.

I had a place to live, and now I was drinking all the time. I got rid
of M and within three months, I was drinking far more than I ever
had when I first started going to AA meetings a decade earlier.

If I had ever doubted that I couldn't have sugar and grains in liquid
form, the next six and a half years proved without a doubt that my
body was like a distillery. Put sugar and grains into it—hard form,
liquid form, it didn't matter—and voilà, there was the phenomenon
of craving that I was powerless over.

I lost a lot of memory and struggled to articulate myself. I would try to explain something and couldn't remember the word to use. It felt as if the word would make it to my tongue and then disappear before I could say it. I'd stumble over my tongue trying to capture the word before it evaporated usually failing to do so.

I couldn't sleep. I learned to read mysteries late into the night or early morning. Since I worked for myself, I changed my hours at my office to afternoons and evenings.

I began to understand the depth and breadth of trauma. In the beginning, everyone comes to help. Churches opened their doors with food, people brought clothes for us, we all felt loved and cared about. We were invited to meals with people in the community who barely knew us. Christmas passed. Then New Year's came and went. And people in the community started moving on with their lives. But we Fire Survivors were stuck. We had no homes of our own and the majority of us were having trouble coming to terms with our insurance companies. It was the start of a long and difficult uphill battle.

Even my best friend's husband said to me at dinner one night, "Sara, you've been down and out for six months. It's time to get over it and get on with your life."

After that, I pulled back from people who hadn't experienced the fire.

FEMA (Federal Emergency Management Agency) gave money for support groups but they didn't last more than a couple of months. I found an ad in the local newspaper asking that anyone interested in joining a support group of Fire Survivors call a private number in Oakland. I called and soon became part of a group of eight women who met once a week for two years. We would share stories of our experiences the day of the fire, of struggling with insurance companies, and the process of choosing architects and contractors for a new house. My best friend, Georgia, was always available for support as well, even though her children were very young.

Meanwhile, I drank. And I drank and drank more. I sought out new friends who had lost homes and who also drank. Like was certainly attracting like.

I was in a situation similar to compulsive eating. I was traumatized. Some therapists would say I was re-traumatized as the few I'd seen considered my childhood traumatic. And while I did seek help, my recovery was hampered by my bingeing and my drinking. And there was a tremendous amount of work to do. My insurance company wanted an inventory of every single thing I owned that had been in the house. I would think about making that list and want to go to bed, all energy escaping out of my little toe. I was grateful for the natural-born leaders, fellow survivors, who invited all of us to meetings at the Claremont Hotel, where they explained what we had to do and why, and answered all our questions. In some cases, they even helped fight insurance companies who were holding out giving replacement money. Because of these heroes in our community, I didn't have to think too much about the next thing to do. But I still had to do the work.

In the years following the fire, I would wonder sometimes if I had learned anything useful from the experience that I could use if something like that ever happened again. In the end, however, I learned only one thing: I could get through it. Period. Being traumatized is ungraceful. People don't understand. They want to understand but they can't without the experience. And often they step on your toes without meaning to.

Being traumatized is another kind of disorder. For me, that disorder was full of depression but not shame. I knew it wasn't my fault that my house had burned down. I was incredibly grateful for the people who had the strength to guide us. It's awful that 3,100 homes had to burn, but I knew that if it had just been my home that had been lost in the fire, and I hadn't had someone telling me exactly what to do and when, I would have been lost. I was nuts, I did nutty things, and even without my eating disorder, some of those things would have been considered insane. But I laughed if someone used the word insane in describing my recovery process from the fire. My addictions were another ballgame altogether. I suffered from so much shame, couldn't understand much less accept my powerlessness, and kept trying to figure it out "on my own."

16
Renewal

Everything about the rebuilding process seemed impossibly hard. In no particular pattern, I felt sorry for myself for being dislocated, exhausted, and traumatized to name just a few feelings. But on the bright side, it was a time of creative growth for me. Also, I was living in a small two-bedroom home on the downhill side of Montclair Village's main street—a lucky break. Not many fire survivors found places as close to their property as I did. The first year after the fire, I was only two blocks south of the burn area. I could be exploring the burned-out remnants of my home in less than fifteen minutes. Living so close only reminded me that the neighborhood looked like a war zone. The second year, however, I was able to be at the building site every day; a real blessing.

As winter moved into spring, a plethora of orange California poppies and purple lupine filled up my entire lot. The seeds had been dropped from helicopters at some point during the winter. As I approached my property, I was greeted by a growing pasture of wildflowers taking back the land that had once been my home. The colors were rich and alive. The half-burned trees that served as a backdrop to this stunning sight looked as if they belonged in this landscape. From the plateau on the land, I looked out on trees that had survived impossible odds. Small green shoots were emerging on large and small trees that were standing side by side with the brick chimneys and stairs that led to nowhere. Six months had passed, and no one in my immediate neighborhood had started rebuilding yet. Spring was competing with the black and rust-orange dirt for drama.

Many of the larger insurance companies resisted paying out the many claims being presented. The last company to settle, Allstate, finally had to give up fighting us after they brought in lawyers to explain why they could only pay such-and-such amount. The lawyers had no idea how to read and interpret the small print in our contracts. Allstate had gathered about five hundred of us in a convention center in downtown Oakland. When the lawyers admitted how baffled they were, we looked at each other, wondering, *Can this be real?*—then slowly realized we had won. We walked out of the center shaking our heads and grinning at the same time.

By the end of August 1992, I had been given enough money to rebuild my home and furnish it. The relief I felt at having completed the difficult task of taking on a giant insurance company was huge— so huge that I threw myself a party, "a blessing of my land," on the property itself.

I took a month to contemplate the pros and cons of rebuilding versus buying a new house but decided to rebuild after looking at ten homes I didn't think I could ever feel comfortable in. I asked an architect friend of mine, Bruce, if he would design a new home for me. My five-year-old goddaughter told me I had to build a cement house so that it wouldn't burn again; she didn't know that nothing survives a 2,000-degree fire unless it's an underground bunker. That said, I liked her idea, and we implemented concrete into the new design. I wanted the look of two very important places in my life— Santa Fe, where my great aunt Sara, who I was named after, lived, and Italy, where I had spent one of the happiest years of my college life.

"I'll see what I can do, but I think I can create something you'll like," Bruce said.

"This is silly," I told him, "but I want one thing more."

"Just tell me and I'll decide if it's silly," he said. "That's my job."

"I want a garage," I said sheepishly. "People have garages to store things in! I want one of those."

Bruce laughed. "A garage it is!"

A month later, Bruce presented me with designs for a house that, waterfall-like, descended down the grade, each floor looking like a separate box. Passersby would call it the Box House after it was finished. I hated that moniker. It stopped once the foliage all grew back and there was so much more to look at than brand-new houses.

After he drew up the plans, Bruce recommended a contractor, someone he had worked with before. "He's good and he charges reasonable prices," he told me.

Before I contacted him, though, I shared the blueprints with a woman designer.

"Is your architect a man?' she asked.

"Yes, why?"

"He has your washer and dryer down in the garage, three flights of stairs. No woman would ever design something like that. Take this back to him and ask him to make space upstairs for the washer and dryer."

I took the designs back to Bruce and he agreed. In the years to come, as I did my laundry on the same floor as my bedroom, I would give thanks to that woman on multiple occasions.

Autumn turned to winter and the contractor didn't want to break ground until February. I made new friends, people who had also lost homes in the fire. People who drank a lot yet made a good living, who had summer homes and would invite me to join them on long weekends. I visited interior design stores and went on tours of beautiful homes to get ideas.

One such tour was a fund-raiser for the French-American School in Berkeley. I visited eight kitchens on that tour, one of which jumped out at me as the perfect kitchen. The home had that Italian/Tuscan look I loved so much and the kitchen had a rustic yet completely finished feeling. The designer's name and number were in the kitchen tour brochure. I called her up and it turned out she and her husband owned the home.

"I was on the kitchen tour this past weekend and I loved your home," I told her. "I also lost my home in the fire and am just getting started rebuilding. I wonder if I could hire you. Bring my plans over and get some feedback or suggestions."

"Of course," she said, "come tomorrow morning. I'd be happy to help. I'll show you the rest of the house if you'd like."

Yes, I'd like!

I showed her my plans the next day, and she told me how to make the outside of the house look like adobe, how to build planters into the wall using half a plastic flower pot, and that by turning the half-pot upside down, I could create light covers.

She also suggested creating nooks on the inside—some large, some small, but all on a scale to showcase little treasures and some large enough to house my speakers.

I left her home feeling, for the first time in a number of years, a sense of creativity—a sense that I didn't have to stand by as an observer in the building process but could become an active member of the team. By the time the house was built, some part of me was in every room, every nook and cranny. It was MY home in a way the home that burned down never had been.

We broke ground February 1993. The foundation was poured first, followed by the bones of the house, the wooden two-by-fours that would hold the house in place. The house seemed to go up in record time. I later learned that the foundation and walls go up fastest. Soon there followed a long period of time where work on the inside of the house was being done. From the outside, it looked as if all work had stopped.

In my small support group of women, I learned that women—both single people like me and wives—were largely responsible for overseeing the construction taking place to rebuild our homes. We were already vulnerable after the trauma of the fire, and a strange thing started happening because of the intimacy of working so closely with the men heading their building crews: the women started talking about having crushes on the men and their growing anxiety about it. The head of my crew was a married man, but I'd be willing to bet that he spent far more time with me than with his wife or family. We were creating together, building together. It would have been easy to fall in love.

It didn't happen for me because I was already having an affair—with alcohol.

I was drinking more and more, sometimes starting as early as my lunch break. My rationale (there is always a rationale for an addict) was that this was a strange time, not a real time. It was a similar feeling to being in an airport or up in a plane. I wasn't really in my life, so the drinking really didn't count. And, to the best of my ability, I was sticking my head in the sand whenever I thought about my food bingeing.

According to Hindu mythology, there was a time long ago when all men were gods. Brahma, chief of the gods, felt that man had abused his divinity and, deciding to take it away, brought all his peers together for a council on where to hide man's divinity.

"Let's bury it at the bottom of the ocean," one of the gods said.

"No. Man will just learn to dive and eventually find it."

"How about deep within the earth?" another offered.

"No. Man will just keep digging until they dig it up."

"Well" said a third, "let's put it at the top of the highest mountain." Brahma thought about it, but said, "Man is smart and will learn to climb even the highest of mountains."

They were all baffled. Then Brahma said, "I have the answer. We'll hide it inside each and every person. They will dig and dive and climb but it will never occur to them to look within themselves to find what they are looking for."

And that's what they did.

For the two years of rebuilding and aftermath of the Oakland firestorm of 1991, I stopped searching for solutions. In December 1993, ten months after breaking ground, I moved into the in-law apartment of my brand-new home. I was moving home. Unlike the old house, which had had a cottage behind the main house, the in-law was attached to the main house. It was the "box" closest to the driveway. It had a separate entrance and because of the grade, no walls in the in-law were the same as any of the walls in my part of the house. I had wanted to be smart, forward-thinking—to plan ahead to when I might sell the house. My thinking was that if a single family bought it from me, they could knock down non-structural walls to turn it into a single-family dwelling. But that would be far in the future, if it happened at all.

Just as in Saint-Exupery's *Little Prince*, where the prince learned to care for his rose and loved it over all other roses, so I loved my new home. I had poured into it all the love and care I had, and a lot of hard work. I had waxed all the knotty pine doors before they were hung. I had helped mix the plaster that had become the walls in the house. I had supervised making all the corners in the house rounded instead of the normal ninety-degree sharp angles that are in most homes. I had shopped for carpeting for the bedrooms and for the light oak planks that became the flooring in the main room that was a combination living room/dining room. I had hired a landscaper to put in gardens before things were anywhere near finished so no damage would be done to the new dwelling while the garden was installed. I had shopped for Mexican tiles for the bathrooms and facsimile limestone tiles that reminded me of the floors and stairs in the magnificent old Florentine houses I remembered for my entryway. I watched over the making of my nooks and the installation of my planters that would be attached to the outside walls. With every new thing I did, I made it more mine.

By early January of 1994, the house was ready for me to move into. After that, my life calmed down, but I was so used to the adrenaline rush of building and creating that I found it very difficult to adjust to ordinary everyday structure. I had time on my hands that I hadn't experienced in over two years. I filled the extra time with drinking and bingeing. My mind sought out memories from before the fire, and I found myself imagining sitting in a meeting of Alcoholics Anonymous, listening to people share their stories at the deepest, most vulnerable level they could dig down into. I missed identifying with those feelings and feeling part of like-minded people. I had nowhere where I felt safe enough to share or discuss the challenging ups and downs of rebuilding my life. I was in one-on-one therapy, and I attended a wonderful therapy group, but the nature of therapy is to get feedback, to comb through one's feelings and actions and learn from one's mistakes. In AA meetings, people just listen to each other. Cross-talk is discouraged to keep the rooms safe so that people can share on a deep level without shame or fear of criticism.

In AA meetings, I had felt one amongst many. I identified. I belonged. Everything I had sought for all my life was available to me in a meeting of Alcoholics Anonymous. It had been at least six years since I'd been to a meeting and, as with many other things·in my life, I hadn't appreciated what was right in front of me until it was no longer there. I longed to be part of that community again, but I didn't want to stop drinking.

For a short time, I had become part of a different community—the community of Fire Survivors. Then I'd become part of the family/ team building my new home. Slowly, these temporary landing places started falling away, and I was left with me and all my self-centered feelings of insecurity.

I started attending Sunday services at different churches and different denominations around the Bay Area. I called myself a seeker, thinking that was a positive word. I liked the minister, Jim Little, at the Lafayette-Orinda Presbyterian Church. I attended just to hear him talk. When he spoke, I really listened. His words struck a chord deep within me. I considered becoming a Presbyterian because of him, and when I made an appointment to talk with him, he listened carefully as I told him an abbreviated version of my life, of searching for a touchstone to hang on to. I left out the information that I was alcoholic and belonged in AA.

When I was finished, Jim leaned in closer to me and said, "The Presbyterian faith is a very intellectual faith. I don't think you'll find here what you are searching for. I don't think you want to talk *about* spirituality, you want to live it, to feel it is the path you walk. You can have that, but not here, I'm afraid."

Was I relieved? Was I disappointed? I don't remember. I was so struck by the fact that he had really heard me and by how honest he was. He cared more about pointing me in a better direction than adding to his flock. Not too long after our talk, he got very sick and another minister took his place on Sunday mornings. It wasn't the same place. What I'd been thinking of as Presbyterian was, in fact, this extraordinary man and his ability to connect with the hearts in his congregation. With him no longer there, the extraordinary became ordinary.

My interlude with the Lafayette-Orinda Presbyterian Church was just another temporary resting place on my road back to Alcoholics Anonymous. Just as a doctor removes all the things that an illness is not before he makes a final diagnosis, so I was removing all the books, places, and people that I thought were the spirituality I needed on my way back to myself. I knew deep down what was wrong. I knew the diagnosis, and I knew the solution. I knew where to go to find everything I was seeking.

I wasn't ready. I got involved with Vipassana meditation and the teachings of Ondrea and Steven Levine. In the end, I did learn to sit still for long periods of time. But food was always on my mind and in my way.

On meditation retreats, we were only to eat two meals a day. Once, I attended a daylong retreat with Jack Kornfield at Spirit Rock in its early days. Jack is an American monk who studied the Vipassana tradition of meditation in Burma. He founded Barre, the retreat center on the East Coast, and was now on the West Coast consulting with the building of Spirit Rock in Marin. Among other things, he was teaching us to taste our food, enjoy our food, be present with our food. He gave us each a couple of raisins (pure sugar for me). We were to put one at a time into our mouths and chew it until it was completely liquid. Then swallow it. We weren't to eat the next raisin until we had completely finished the one before.

I sat in a crowd of people at Spirit Rock, which was just a few tents at the time. Jack sat in a chair at the front of our group. We sat facing him surrounded by trees, a blue cloudless sky and the quiet that fifty people can find only at a meditation retreat. I looked around me to see what others were doing. I felt like a total imposter. I couldn't enjoy the raisin. I wanted more. I was living in a future where I could get more. Who were these people around me who could chew just one raisin?

I wanted to cry. I wanted to eat all the raisins.

I left the retreat that day feeling utterly alone, completely unteachable, and wondering, *Why can't I be like other people?*

Though I was steeped in self-pity and misery, I kept resisting the short walk to my nearest twelve-step meeting. Sometimes I find myself shaking my head at the enormous amount of energy I used to avoid returning to AA. What would it have looked like if I had accepted my disease and put all that energy into my recovery? A useless machination, I'm told. Alcoholics love to say, "It takes what it takes to get here."

Nothing ever worked the way I thought it should. As always, I would think I'd found an answer and then end up feeling like I was in that glass bell jar looking out at satisfied, peaceful people while I was hurting, lonely, and feeling hopeless on the inside.

By 1998, I had been living in my new home longer than I'd lived in the home that burned down. I was working full time again. I felt like a real "grown-up." I had money set aside from the insurance claim, and my garden had been landscaped and planted. I had a view of the Bay and the Golden Gate Bridge from my bedroom window. I was learning about baseball and that I could scream and yell at baseball games and get out tons of energy. That gave me an outlet for a lot of uncomfortable feelings. On the outside, my life was looking more and more like a really privileged life. But on the inside, I harbored every possible miserable resentment and feeling that made me a drunk, a food addict, and a selfish child.

I had many new friends I'd met in the years after the fire. The ones I liked the best were the ones I drank with. I used to say about one couple I spent a lot of time with that I wasn't sure what was more important to them: oxygen or alcohol. They poured wine freely and often. They were creative, adored rock and roll as I did, had me over for dinner a lot, and seemed to think of me as family. That cocktail was irresistible to me.

I had started entertaining in my home. In spite of my "poor me" attitude, I knew I was fortunate to have emerged from the firestorm intact and owning a beautiful home. On May 31, 1998, I threw a huge party and invited everyone I knew.

That morning, I started preparations. I had become a regular customer at Costco. There, I could buy massive amounts of wine and hard liquor for half of what I would spend otherwise. Laden with plenty of Chianti, I started drinking early as I stood in my kitchen. By the time people were arriving around 5:00 p.m., I was pleasantly drunk. I sat out on the patio, off my kitchen, and stayed there the entire party. I found it too hard to make the rounds. My friends had to come out to talk to me. I definitely was not the hostess with the mostest. I pulled myself together with great effort in order to say good-bye to most of my guests. Two people stayed on. I hadn't seen one of them in years. I pulled out a bottle of scotch, and we sat on my living room floor drinking most of it. I made it to my bed and passed out.

Around six in the morning, I woke up. I lay there with the same old, very tired, very well-worn-out phrase haranguing me: *You've done it again. How could you?* Only this time, the answer was not a self-inflicted inner berating. I heard an internal voice say loud and clear, "Sara, this elevator only goes down. It goes to the basement. You can get out now or on any floor you choose."

I had heard that expression many times in the AA meetings I'd gone to in the '80s. I'd always thought of it as advice and wisdom passed on from one alcoholic to another. Apparently it had metabolized, because here it was, deep within me. As I awoke June 1, it seemed to come out of nowhere. If it's true that one's Higher Power resides within, it was surely a piece of wisdom that, fully awake, I was incapable of hearing. Something wise inside of me knew that I'd only listen if I was half awake. I lay there in a state of part hangover, part thoughtfulness, and I somehow knew not to question what I was hearing. I was finished. I'd had enough liquor for many lifetimes.

I didn't realize how done I was until much later. For that moment, what I heard was, "It's up to you. Stop drinking now or keeping going down."

In my life, I have had a few moments like these—moments where the fog lifted and I knew the right thing to do to care for myself. Too often, I've let them pass me by. I'm not clear why I grabbed this moment, this precious moment, but I like to think that I found the divinity within me and finally paid attention.

Over the next couple of days, all the things I had learned over the prior fifteen years came flowing back, and I found I was willing to embrace them.

I knew, beyond a doubt, that if I was going to stay sober, I couldn't do it alone, so I called my old Greysheet sponsor, Sarah D, who was writing her PhD dissertation in Los Angeles. I asked her if I could drive down to Los Angeles to visit her. I had only seen her a handful of times in the last several years, but she said, "Of course."

Still ashamed to show up at a meeting in the Bay Area, I drove to LA on Friday, June 5, with four days of sobriety. I knew Sarah cared about me and wouldn't judge me. She was renting a small home in Westwood while doing research at the Getty Library. I stayed for two nights but didn't tell her that I had been drinking right up until Sunday morning before. Shame is a strange companion. It taught me to be afraid of people who would actually help me and to trust people who would hurt me. Shame doesn't allow for good judgment. It taught me fear, and fear caused me to be wrong about most everything.

Though I'd known Sarah for fifteen years, knew that she wouldn't judge and would be quick to help me, I was still afraid of telling her. I put it off by having her tell me all about her for the first twenty-four hours. She took me to the Getty Library and showed me where her little office was.

The Getty was new to Los Angeles. There was still a Getty Museum in Malibu, but much of the valuable work had been transferred to the new library. Sarah pointed me toward different areas to explore, then left me on my own while she worked.

I wandered the gardens, which had yet to bloom. Small plantings peeked out of brown sacking cloth. A little color appeared here and there, just enough to give me a sense that in ten years' time these gardens would be magnificent. I was standing high on a hill above Los Angeles. I could see 360 degrees around me. To the west was the coast and the Pacific Ocean. South was traffic filling in every possible roadway that led to downtown LA. East was a flat scenario of homes without end, the suburbs of LA that eventually gave way to the desert. And north, the grapevine stretch of I-5 snaked its way over the hills out of the LA basin and into the vast, long emptiness of central California. All this was only slightly marred by the famous LA smog.

The library building itself stood at the top of long, wide steps that seemed to rise all together incrementally to reach the front door. I went inside and walked around. Much of the library was closed off to me, a guest and spectator. It was a research library that welcomed people like Sarah to come for a month or two at a time to do the kind of art history research that only a place like the Getty can provide. What was available to the public was a small exposition of what they called illuminated manuscripts with their beautifully illustrated first letters. Pages were on display. They looked to be from the Middle Ages and the Renaissance. I looked at each one carefully, in awe of the patience it took to create such a detailed illustration.

When Sarah and I met up again, she asked me what I thought.

"Will the inside stage more and larger expos?" I asked. "I actually think the building and its location is the real attraction."

"Probably not," she said, "but who knows. The Getty Foundation has so much money that they can buy whatever they want. They need to keep buying in order to spend the amount of money that has been mandated by the family."

"Can you imagine having so much money that you have to buy beautiful works of art!" I marveled. "What a concept."

The next morning, Sunday morning, I forced myself to tell Sarah that I had been drinking alcoholically for six and a half years. We were in her living room, still in our pajamas and finishing up breakfast. She looked at me and said, "Get dressed. We're going to a meeting."

I was ready to do what I was told.

There was a large meeting close by. Confessing to Sarah that I had been drinking was one thing. Standing up and telling a hundred or more strangers was another. I felt like I was five years old, hiding behind a mythical mother's skirts. I would peek out and then hide again. I wasn't shy, I was terrified.

The people Sarah introduced me to were welcoming and kind. There was nothing to be afraid of; I was the only one judging me.

Most everyone there was clearly healthy and happy. When the meeting started and the leader asked if there were any newcomers, I kept my mouth shut. I wasn't ready to go to any lengths. Was I desperate enough to get sober?

It turned out I was but for the next couple of years, I would do it the hard way. And at this first meeting, Sarah didn't try to get me to do anything that I wasn't willing to do. It was enough that I had come.

I listened to two speakers, two men who between them had about eighty years of sobriety. Everything was just as I remembered. One of the speakers made fun of the way his mind tried to rationalize why he should keep drinking. The audience laughed. We'd all been there. I'd been there, but wasn't quite far enough removed to be able to laugh at myself.

Halfway through the meeting, Sarah took my hand. "You're in the right place," she told me.

Before I started my trip back to Oakland, I finally talked told Sarah everything. While she listened, just as had happened fifteen years earlier, she didn't make false promises. She didn't send me off with, "You're going to be okay." We both knew I had a lot of hard work ahead to stay sober. I'd let the disease back in the door once. I knew how baffling and powerful it was. Now I needed to ask for human help and spiritual help.

17

Crossroads of Desperation and Hope

For the next five years I worked the AA program religiously. I was completely committed. This time, I took the program seriously. I got a sponsor, and then, when she wanted to be a friend more than be an example of recovery, I asked another person. I took on service positions.

I still did silly things, like choosing recovering alcoholics for my boyfriends. It's only looking back that I comprehend how broken we all are when we first come into those rooms. We hear brutal stories of near death, imprisonment, and reminders of the hell of being held captive by the disease of alcoholism. I forgave myself for looking for comfort and love in all the wrong places. As long as I stayed sober, the promise was that I would grow out of my immaturity, my stunted growth.

There was still an unease in me, though. I was back in one fold but still trying to deal with my food addiction on my own. I thought, *Maybe I can do this in AA and not have to go back to OA.* As I had been told very often, however, these programs are *we* programs. *We* do it together because *I* cannot do it alone. I had to have like-minded food addicts in recovery for talk, support, and experience, and to grasp on to their hope and strength until I felt my own. I had to hear over and over that what I had was not a little problem with food and weight but a serious, life-and-death disease of addiction. It was clear I couldn't remember it on my own. Yet I was depriving myself of life-saving support because I was too ashamed to admit that fact and too afraid to return, thinking I'd be harshly criticized.

In those last years of the '90s and the first half of the '00s, my disorder took on an air of predictability. I was terrified of feeling. And success in the first couple of years in AA meant feeling lots of feelings—some I was totally unacquainted with and some I'd spent a lifetime trying to avoid. I often felt that my nerve endings had burst through my skin. Everything I bumped into, both metaphorically and literally, felt so painful. I shopped at very small, expensive food markets where there were fewer people to interact with and bump up against.

But I still thought I should go to all AA events that I was able to attend no matter how big. We had First Friday potluck speaker meetings. I'd often walk into the large meeting room full of "free-floating anxiety," and it wouldn't take much for me to be so uncomfortable that I couldn't stand to be there. Watching a couple that looked close and in love; arriving after a unpleasant phone call; being exhausted after work; all these served as triggers for bingeing.

Now that I wasn't drinking, I'd returned to my bottom-line solution for escaping from my feelings—food—and there was plenty to be had. Tables overflowed with huge quantities of food that members had brought. I usually white-knuckled it until after the speaker had finished, although I spent the whole time thinking about every single morsel of food sitting on those tables. I then planned the binge. First, I rationalized why just one of something would be okay. I made it over to the dessert table and filled a paper plate full of chocolate chip cookies, candies, brownies, and ice cream if it was there. Then I ate it, first slowly pretending I was a normal eater, then gorging. I wanted more. No matter that I already had more on the plate—I wanted MORE. The whole table.

If you've ever watched a movie where a man turns into a werewolf, that is what I felt like. I was transforming into a monster in front of all my friends. I thought they were all looking at me. I had to get out of there. I'd get in the car with my "stash" and drive, regardless of how much food I already had with me, to the supermarket. I'd go home, eat my stash, realize immediately that it wasn't nearly enough, and then head back out to the market to buy more cookies and more ice cream.

Once home, I felt safe, but, in fact, by myself, I was in the worst company I could possibly be in. If people couldn't see me, I could eat as I pleased. In the ensuing trance, I'd tell myself that I could handle anything, but this was the farthest thing from the truth. I was drunk on food. And I was supposedly in recovery.

This scene played out in many ways over the next seven years. AA suggests that recovering alcoholics practice total honesty. I was trying, really trying, but I was also hanging on to my huge blind spot. I was no longer ingesting sugar and grains in liquid form, but I refused to admit that I couldn't ingest them in any form. I knew this, had known it, for years. But I wanted to believe that now that I was sober from alcohol, I would no longer practice my other addictions.

My experience was like a game of Whack-A-Mole. Push down one addiction and up popped another. Food was my bottom-line addiction. I turned to alcohol when I tried to control the food. I turned to speed when I tried to lose weight. I smoked cigarettes because it was cool. I bit my nails down to the quick, until they bled, because I hated my life so much. I stole money to buy food. I lied when I was caught stealing. I hung out with people as low on the totem pole as me so I wouldn't notice how abnormal my behavior was. And always, always there was food. It wasn't illegal to eat. It wasn't illegal to binge.

And I couldn't seem to eat without bingeing unless I was drinking or smoking or up to no good.

Now, I was sober. I had stopped smoking cigarettes. I had new friends and I was learning to act like a real grown-up. I wasn't stealing. And for the most part, I had stopped lying—except to myself—about how much food I was eating. I had what I would describe as a rocky sobriety. It felt good to go to meetings and hang out with other alcoholics. It felt wonderful to be able to laugh at the horrible things that all alcoholics seem to do. I loved going to parties and having a good time without alcohol. But it also felt incredibly lonely being in that crowd with my huge secret—that I was a food addict. I had convinced myself that one disease was okay, but two? I was ashamed and imagined no one would want to be my friend if they knew the truth.

A few important things happened that pushed me closer to the precipice of choosing between the "known" disease: bingeing and the "unknown."

First was the experience of going home for Thanksgiving in 2005 with my mother and cousin, Elizabeth. Elizabeth and I had traveled to Philadelphia, me from Oakland, Elizabeth from Memphis. We were sharing a guest apartment at Pennswood Village where my mother was still living. She was now ninety-two years old, and while she still looked younger than her years, her frailty was showing, especially when she walked. She used a walker and an electric cart. I sometimes teased her that she was going to get a traffic ticket the way she went speeding around the halls of Pennswood.

For a while, maybe eight months, she hadn't seemed herself. Her memory was worse than usual. She'd forget from one phone call to another that she was angry with me. (I would learn about a year later that she'd had a couple of minor strokes and had also fallen out of bed a number of times, but her pride wouldn't let her tell anyone. It was Anna, her nurse companion of many years, who eventually let me know.) Mom did not want to have to leave her apartment and move to assisted living. In addition to her physical ailments, she was wound up tight all the time.

We had a calm Thanksgiving dinner with a couple of her friends. The dinner was full of interesting conversation, which my mother thrived on. All seemed to be going well.

The next day, Elizabeth and I found our way into central Philadelphia using public transportation. Elizabeth had never seen the Liberty Bell, and Philadelphia had had a major makeover since I'd last seen it. We visited the Arch Street meeting house, the first Quaker meeting house in the US. Although it was midday on a Friday, it was open, and a kind elderly man came to talk to us. I told him I'd been raised Quaker, mostly at the Radnor meeting, west of Philly. I felt so sad when he told me that every year, there were fewer and fewer members of the Contemplative Quaker faith. Long before I'd ever heard of twelve-step programs, the Quakers, through my summer camp, through the Princeton meeting house, had fed my soul. That had been a constant in my life. Being a Quaker wasn't enough to cure me of my addictions, but they would have been the first to say, "Go get help. We can do a lot and we can support you, but we aren't equipped to deal with your addiction."

Back at Pennswood, my mother was having a temper tantrum. She had forgotten that we had gone into Philadelphia and couldn't understand where we'd disappeared to. The minute we stepped onto the Pennswood grounds, several people told me, "Your mother is looking for you. She is very upset."

The more powerless she felt, the angrier she got.

When I walked into her room, she flew into a full-blown rage.

"WHERE . . . HAVE . . . YOU . . . BEEN?" Her body was quivering. My mother was no longer tall; she had shrunk to my height. I outweighed her by thirty or forty pounds. But at that moment, I was standing next to a giant who was breathing fire down at me. I felt really scared.

"We went to Philadelphia. I told you last night that we were going and that we'd see you for dinner." Because Elizabeth was standing next to me, I was able to keep my voice much calmer than I felt.

"You did not. I have looked everywhere for you. I've called everyone that you know here at Pennswood. I was so embarrassed saying I'd lost my daughter. How could you do that to me? When will you ever grow up?"

I just stood there, trying not to cry. Through years of therapy, I'd learned it was useless to keep defending myself. She had no desire for an explanation or a discussion.

"I've had enough of you and your behavior," she berated me. "You said you want to visit and spend time with me but you don't. You just want to continue your self-centered ways. I've had it. I'm too old to put up with this. I thought I'd have a heart attack today. I don't want you coming back here—ever."

Elizabeth didn't say a word. Years later, she told me that she'd never seen that side of my mother. She was stunned and speechless.

My mother had never before wanted to talk about anything or hear another side of a story. At ninety-two, she wasn't about to change her stripes. I felt that if I opened my mouth it would only seem provocative. So I said nothing at all.

I returned to Oakland feeling bankrupt of all spiritual forgiveness— either for myself or her. I had seven years in AA, but that day when I returned to Oakland, I felt as empty and bereft as I ever had. This time I knew enough to ask for help, and my sponsor suggested that I check myself into a treatment center as a preventative measure—a shot in the arm, a place where I could rest and listen to other people's stories of recovery. She told me that in her thirty-five years of sobriety, she had watched two husbands die. Both times she fell apart, she hadn't been able to cope and had wanted to die.

"My sponsor told me the same thing I'm telling you," she said. "Take a week to get away from the world. Not staying sober just wasn't an option for me when I lost my husbands, and the treatment center helped me remember that my sobriety is the most important thing in my life, that I can get through loss and not drink."

I was ready to hear her advice. I wanted to curl up somewhere and not have to do anything. I wanted to be protected from myself and my disease. I didn't want to drown in my self-pity or in food.

I started researching recovery centers near me and found that even with all their fancy advertising, they didn't have much that attracted me. I just wanted plain, honest recovery. Eventually I chose Hazelden, which was not close to me at all but an hour east of St. Paul, Minnesota. Hazelden had a positive track record. The vast percentage of people there were newly sober, but there were also people like me who had some years and wanted a "tune-up". For that, they had created a place and a program called the Lodge. Anyone from any twelve-step program could come and stay at the Lodge, a separate building a ten-minute walk from the main center. I made plans to spend the week between Christmas and New Year's there. I started to look forward to it, to the possibility that there was something that might quiet all the voices in my head and help me turn all that energy in a positive direction.

Earlier that autumn, before I'd resolved to go to Hazelden, I had planned a trip to Brazil for mid-January 2006. On December 16, I went into San Francisco to apply for and pick up my visa for the trip. By complete chance, while I was wandering around waiting for the consulate to process my papers, I ran into Isabelle, my best friend from my years in Overeaters Anonymous. Neither of us lived in San

Francisco anymore. We hadn't seen each other in ten years. In fact, the last time I'd seen her she'd been very heavy and ashamed about her weight. Now she looked like a person transformed. She was her normal body weight. She seemed radiant, glowing.

She was as happy to see me as I her. She gave me a huge hug and whispered, "You'll never guess what I'm doing."

"What?" I responded excitedly.

"Greysheet. I'm so sorry I teased you about it back then. It's saving my life, just like you said it would. I have three and a half years of abstaining from sugar, grains, and carbos."

"You're kidding. Where do you go to meetings?"

"In Albany."

We talked some more and promised to stay in touch. I went home after picking up my visa and looked around my kitchen. A small spark had ignited in me. I wanted what Isabelle had. I still had my scale, my little spatulas and measuring cups. I searched my fridge and my cupboards. I found canned tuna. I cooked up some carrots. I chopped up other vegetables. I was making myself an abstinent dinner, which meant no refined carbs, sugar, or grains and also meant weighing it on the scale. It was like getting back on a horse after a bad fall. It was easy.

I did the same thing at breakfast the next day. I found foods that had no sugar, grains, or carbohydrates. I weighed them on my scale and then had a meal that was free of wondering if I was going to gain weight, free from planning a binge, free of stress. I did the same thing at lunch and at dinner. I called Isabelle and pretended that I was just asking after her welfare and reiterated how wonderful it was to run in to her. I'm sure she saw through my pretense but she was kind enough to play along. I really wanted some of her recovery to seep into me by osmosis, but I couldn't yet ask her for help. I wanted to beg "Please help me!" but the words just wouldn't come out of my mouth. I was acting so very interested in her, and all I really wanted was for her to think I was doing just fine, thank you. I still equated asking for help with being weak, with being a bad person.

On Sunday, after three more meals of weighing exactly what I was going to eat and staying away from sugar, grains, and refined carbohydrates, I called her again. This time, I asked her to be my sponsor.

"Maybe, Sara," she said, a little doubtful. "We've been close friends in the past, though, and that's not recommended, as you know."

"I do know, but I trust you," I said to her.

I heard a chuckle. "Okay, let's try it on a temporary basis. We can decide if it's working after a month."

A month? It was a miracle that I hadn't binged in three days. But I said, "Okay, that's good."

"But Sara . . ."

"Yes?"

"You have to do what I tell you. I mean it. You are just like me and think your way is better. I'm here to tell you that your way does not work—in case you are still under any illusion. It never did, and it never will."

She didn't have to convince me. I was fifty-eight years old and not a single thing, with the exception of the five months I was following the program written on that grey sheet of paper in 1983, had ever worked. I had a window of opportunity here, and I was seeing myself clearly. Isabelle called it the crossroads of desperation and hope. It was my choice. My seven years in AA made the right choice possible.

Not only was I not drinking now, I was also working hard to be honest with myself, to take my head out of the sand no matter how hard it was, no matter how much it hurt, and see the truth that had always been right in front of me. With sobriety and willingness, I had allowed myself to ask for help. I had known for years that this grey sheet of paper was the only thing that worked for me. With gentleness and love, Isabelle held my hand and guided me back to the solution for addictive eating. I grabbed it with every ounce of my being.

I ran into Isabelle on December 16. On Christmas day, nine days later, I flew to St. Paul, Minnesota, and Hazelden Recovery Center. This was my first long stretch of staying abstinent from sugar, grains, and carbohydrates and being away from my kitchen.

I arrived in the late afternoon and was shown my room in the Lodge. There were two twin beds in it. My host told me I was lucky; everyone usually got a roommate at the Lodge, but because of the time of year, I'd be getting a single. The room was pleasant—big enough to house two women for a week—but I was glad I didn't have to find out whether I'd be a good roommate. There was a floor-to-ceiling glass pane that served as the back wall, and through it I could see the winter garden and cardinals in the trees. California doesn't get cardinals, and I'd always associated them with Christmas, so it felt just perfect that I would get to watch them out my window each day.

I arrived in time for dinner. The cafeteria was located in the same building, not far from the dormitory. After being introduced to two other people who'd be spending the week at the Lodge, we stood in line like elementary school kids. We were served our dinner by a tall man wearing a hair net and a white jacket, just as if he was in an upscale restaurant. I had my scale with me and when it came to be my turn to be served, I put the scale on top of the glass ledge that separated him from me.

"I need to weigh my food," I said to him, and put an institutional white plate on the scale. Then I held my breath, not sure what he would say or do.

"All your food, or just some?" he asked. "How much do you need?"

Really? No questions asked?

He saw the relief on my face. "Don't worry," he said. "We support all the twelve-step programs. I'm Tom. You just come and let me know if you need anything."

I had been prepared for a long explanation of why it was necessary, why I was different.

I was prepared to do battle with my mother. But it wasn't necessary. With Tom, what I did with my food was no big deal. With him helping me, I was sure I could make it through the week without too much trouble.

The week went far too fast. Each morning, when we woke up, the handful of us staying at the Lodge would meet in the living room, which had lots of comfortable couches and chairs and a coffee table with AA literature on it. As was recommended, someone would volunteer to read a short but inspiring piece from the literature, and we'd share any experience that it brought up for each one of us. This was all self-led, and a grounding, thoughtful start to the day. It set me on a daily path of wanting to learn more, to get emotionally healthier. I went to breakfast, our next part of the morning, feeling full and expansive.

The buffet line at meals was never long, as there were so few of us at the Lodge. Behind the glass, Tom, our tall, gracious server smiled every time he saw me. I would put my scale up on the counter and he would slowly put food on my plate until I asked him to stop. I kept waiting for the other shoe to drop. But he didn't seem put out that it had to be exact—not one-eighth of an ounce over or under. I had no experience with this kind of support. It felt like a gift of love.

The rest of the day was devoted to group meetings, some that were more lecture than a sharing experience and some that resembled an AA meeting. The grounds were filled with dirty snow, and my cardinal appeared daily outside of my window.

Hazelden is about an hour east of the Twin Cities, an area where there is nothing but flat land stretching out forever. My overall impression was of greyness. The sky was grey, the snow was a cinder grey. There wasn't much to distract us from the reason we were all there: a shot in the arm of the spiritual experience that is Alcoholics Anonymous and the twelve-step way of life.

Only once did one of the counselors try to talk me out of doing the Greysheet program because, even though he personally had no experience with food addiction, he thought he knew a program that might be better for me. This was based on an experience he'd had with another woman who'd attended one of these weeklong stays a few months before me. She was a member of a branch of OA: OA HOW (Honesty, Openness, Willingness). The counselor saw that it worked for her and wanted to pass it on to me.

This was when I realized how committed I was to my Greysheet program. In my heart, I knew that I had done all the research on all the programs, all the diets, all the possibilities out there for a food addict such as myself, and I had an absolute conviction that Greysheet was right for me. I was a binger who had no on/off button, so weighing and measuring my food, without exception, took away any chance of my trying to get more food. I was a liar and a cheat with myself, so if I wanted to be successful, the only way was to write down my food and commit it to a sponsor. It was so much easier to be honest with someone else other than with myself. Being accountable to another food addict worked. (It helped that that other person was Isabelle, someone I admired and trusted. I had always thought of her as a sensible, grounded person.)

There was no doubt in my mind that I was addicted to sugar, grains, and simple carbohydrates. If I didn't eat those substances, I had no physical cravings and could work to change my attitude about living in this world. And, as if all of that wasn't enough, I felt good. In fact, I felt great. After only two weeks of following the Greysheet program—exactly as it was written, with no tweaks on my part—the fog was clearing from my head. I was feeling energy. I was feeling calmer. I was not experiencing any of the withdrawal symptoms that

I'd had in 1983. (People in addiction recovery say that sugar is as hard to get off of as heroin.)

Best of all, I was feeling full.

The food was good at Hazelden, and that fed my physical needs. The sharing, the companionship of other addicts, and the reminder of how the twelve-step programs work and *why* they work filled me with a hope and love that I hadn't felt in a long time.

This was my first true spiritual experience. I didn't see white lights—nothing extraordinary happened—and yet it was extraordinary. I, who had lived most of my life feeling so sorry for myself, blaming others for all my misfortune, could actually see a future with integrity and space in my heart for others, and where I didn't have to resort to the three amigos (sugar, grains, and refined carbohydrates) to dull my senses and help me escape my pain. As a good friend of mine says, "When we are into our addictions, we only have one problem—how to get abstinent. When we get abstinent, then we have one problem after another, just like normal people out in the world."

I saw this as something to look forward to. I didn't know what my exact future would look like but I was clear that I never had to be alone with these addictions again, and whatever the future held, I was pretty sure that my very worst day would be much better than the hell my addictions had taken me to.

Epilogue

Since that day in December 2005 when I ran into Isabelle, I have had a few stumbles. However, my fear of compulsively bingeing and the fear of returning to and living in that hell of compulsive eating has never wavered. Since May of 2009, when I finally achieved complete acceptance that I had no power over this disease, I have adhered to black-and-white abstinence from sugar, grains and carbohydrates, and in doing so have learned to live in the grey areas of life.

My life today is unrecognizable to the one I lived before 2005. I've always been skeptical of "miracles," but today there is no doubt in my mind that something miraculous has happened. I, who most of my life could barely go a couple of days without bingeing, have not binged or found it necessary to eat sugar, grains, or carbohydrates in years. I have traveled to many countries, taking my food on the plane and making my seatmates jealous of my healthy, abundant meals each time. I have moved to Paris and am living the dream of learning another language, another culture, and experiencing the beauty of this amazing city. I have made friends all over the world that have the same disorder I do. I've learned that I'm not alone with this addiction and do not need to be ashamed that I have it. Being a food addict is not a moral issue. I have an allergy to sugar, grains, and carbohydrates in liquid and hard form. My body doesn't metabolize these things as many people's do; instead, my body turns it all into a poison that sets off the phenomenon of craving, sending the beast off and running. I don't understand how this happens any more than I understand how I was born with brown hair and my sister was born with red hair. It just is. I can fight it, or I can accept it and move on into a life worth living.

The farther away I got from my last binge, the more clearly I saw the disease for what it is: a debilitating illness. I've never thought that denial might serve a good purpose, but, in retrospect, I am grateful that the "fog in my head" and the "blindness in my eyes" didn't all go away at the same time. If I had been suddenly struck totally sane, with the ability to see all the damage I had done, both to myself and others, I don't think I could have stayed abstinent. I started healing first physically, then mentally and emotionally, and finally spiritually. In the beginning, all that was asked of me was to use all the tools at my disposal that helped me to abstain from sugar, grains, and carbohydrates—to protect my abstinence. My most precious tool was my kitchen scale. With the decision already made of how much to eat, I didn't have to do that thinking. The space between my ears started being used for different kinds of thoughts—thoughts that had nothing to do with food or alcohol.

It took two years for me to feel any kind of confidence that what I had found would not be ripped away from me. I had to work at it full time. It was as if I was learning another language. I didn't know how to cook. I didn't know how to plan meals or take a shopping list to the grocery store and stick to the list. I learned to avoid certain aisles in all grocery stores. I had eaten out of boxes, tins, and ice cream cartons for so long that the kitchen had become a place where I just stood with a spoon, vacuuming sugar down as if I hadn't eaten in a week. I had to change my view of the world from that of a self-centered, angry woman to a woman who had gratitude, who embraced others and their point of view. Someone who looked to her side of the street for faults and let others take care of themselves.

It was a slow process for me. All my life I had been counting calories, talking about "legal" versus "illegal" foods, and making my weight the most important thing in my life. I truly believed that if I became thin, all my problems would be solved. Physical health is important, there is no doubt about that. However, I had a lot of work to do on my attitude. I was told by others that had gone ahead of me that without an attitude change, I would eventually fall back into my old ways of thinking and self-destruction. I knew that to be true from my first period of abstinence in 1983.

The most important thing I had to learn was that my eating disorder was an addiction. Like all addictions—alcohol, money, gambling, sex—just wanting to stop was useless. The addiction was too powerful. I had managed to cut countless corners and talk my way in and out of many things in my life, but I was up against something big—and no amount of my tricks or intelligence or trying to will it away was going to be effective. I needed help in the form of other people with the same addiction who had more experience living in the solution. I had reached age fifty-eight trying to heal myself on my own. I didn't need to do any more research. I couldn't fix a broken tool with a broken tool.

The cure for addiction is most often complete abstinence. Food addiction is different. I could abstain completely from sugar, grains, and carbohydrates, but I had to eat. Since I was addicted to "more"— since I was a binger—what I needed were boundaries around food. My fellow food addicts taught me to follow these rules:

1. Eat only three times a day (to lessen the pain of having to stop).

2. Use a scale to weigh out portions of everything (so I didn't have to depend on my broken eyes).

3. Make a commitment to another person. I would detail for them what I would eat for the next three meals. I had always broken every commitment I'd ever made to myself. I was much less likely to break a commitment to another person.

4. Remember that I was sick. I had a disease and no pill was going to cure me. Everything I was doing was the medicine that would make me well.

5. I had to reach out and get to know my fellow addicts by making phone calls and showing up for group meetings.

I had never been successful talking with people about my issues with food. I'd tried therapists but they'd never understood. I'd joined encounter groups in the '70s to "learn to love my body!" I had been to Thin Within, Jenny Craig, and various iterations of Overeaters Anonymous. I'd had urine shots in my butt, eaten boxes and boxes of AYDs ("appetite-suppressant" candies popular back in the late '50s that were supposed to make your stomach feel full; they were just candy to me, and I ate them by the box). If the plan had structure, they didn't believe in addiction. The OA plan didn't stress structure but did believe food addiction was a disease. I truly believe it takes another addict to understand the utter helplessness and despair that comes with food addiction. And that person also has to believe that there is a solution that works in order to provide the necessary hope. I also believe that I never really told the whole truth to anyone. I wanted to hold on to some pretense of being in control. Until I heard that there were people just like me, who did the exact same things with food I did, I didn't really let anyone have enough information to help me.

It turns out that these boundaries, though difficult to learn, were satisfying. I could do "hard." I no longer fell back on my victim mode—"You don't understand, it's so hard for me." In fact, my new friends in Greysheet did understand how hard it was to tame an addiction, and those group members who had gone before me had done it. I was told to make three phone calls a day and get to at least three meetings a week. I craved these specifics. I needed not to have to think about it—just to be told what to do.

I had always thought of boundaries as restrictions and felt I would suffer if I had any placed on me. I believed I would feel deprived. What actually happened was that I felt a huge sense of relief and freedom. I didn't have to wonder what I could and couldn't eat on a daily basis. It had already been figured out for me. I wasn't a special case. I was just a garden-variety food addict who could follow the same food plan that worked for everyone else.

People, sometimes friends, will ask me, "How long do you think you will have to weigh your food?" I don't plan on stopping. There is a cliché that I like very much: "If it ain't broke, don't fix it." Besides, I know what people are really asking me: *When are you going to be cured? When will you be normal?* I now believe that one of the greatest gifts I've gotten from accepting my food addiction is that I have learned to accept myself as I am. I don't have to get "better." I am a woman, I have brown hair, I am a food addict, and I am enough. Everybody has something, it turns out. People who accept their issues and find ways to work with them get on with their lives. Some problems are permanent, and we have to learn to live with them. It's called growing up, maturing.

I no longer think there is something wrong with me. I inherited this disorder, and I have learned how to live with it. I do have to be vigilant, however. Addictions are tricky things. It is a disease that will tell you that you don't have a disease: "Go ahead, have that ice cream. You'll be fine." Finally, I now know that voice is a lie. If I have let it get loud enough that I'm actually listening, I need to take a long, hard look at what's going on in my life. Am I really tired—sleep deprived? Am I lonely—when was the last time I had a nice connection with one of my friends? Am I resentful—pissed off at someone and holding on to it? Any and all of those things can be true at any time. And now I know that if I give in to that voice and eat sugar, it won't solve whatever is out of whack, but it *will* put me back on the path of craziness, weight gain, misery, and self-loathing.

I love ice cream. But I can't think of any flavor or brand of ice cream that is worth giving up what I have today.

My college roommate, Dorothy, and I were walking to a restaurant in New York City when she suddenly blurted out, "This dinner almost didn't happen."

It was evening and already dark. We were just stepping into the crosswalk to cross the street when she said this.

"Why?" I asked her.

"Babs remembers that trip when you didn't tell her you had drugs when the two of you crossed over the Yugoslavian border. She was furious then, and she is furious now. I had to talk her into giving you a chance."

"That was forty years ago," I said. Inside, I was wishing the earth would open up so I could jump in and disappear. Outside, I just kept walking, robot-like.

"Yes, but what you did was bad. You both could have been put in prison for twenty years."

I knew she was right. I'm always getting reminders that my food addiction caused me to act so thoughtlessly that I put my life and others' lives in danger in the past. That is the nature of addiction. Still, it was hard having my bad behavior smacked so suddenly in my face.

"Why is she willing to have dinner with me now?" I asked.

"That's about it, she is willing to give it a try. And she doesn't know I'm telling you this."

Oh god! I wanted to crack a joke, say something stupid and funny to take away my discomfort. But this turned out to be one of those rare times when I stayed with my feelings.

I had done a lot of bad things. I had stolen money, clothing, food out of people's cupboards, and much more. I'd been told that I had to make those things right. I had a list of people and places I needed to make amends to. Babs wasn't on that list. I had completely forgotten what I had done to her, that I had endangered her life just so I could have drugs and be cool with my hippie friends.

I hadn't seen Babs since we were seniors in college, but as soon as I saw her, I knew her. She looked the same. I'd always thought she looked like Vanessa Redgrave. My heart was beating very fast. I was completely at a loss for what to say after, "Hi, it's great to see you again." I had to get through that dinner without letting on that I knew what Babs had told Dorothy. And somehow make amends by acting age appropriate.

While we were drinking coffee after dinner, Babs turned to me and said, "You seem so different. You are calm. You always used to be such a ball of anxiety and nervous energy."

What a nice way of saying that I had been a total selfish jerk who spun through my life and others' lives like a tornado. I couldn't have asked for a higher compliment. That I even passed as an adult was due to all those people who'd gone before me and been my cheerleaders when, day after day, I ate only my weighed meals. It belonged to the people who'd answered the phone and let me wail away about how hard this recovery was, how so-and-so had done me wrong. It belonged to the founders of Alcoholics Anonymous, who'd been the first people to guarantee that people like me could stop practicing their addictions—if we followed a few simple guidelines.

I was calm that evening. The shame I felt evaporated with her comment. This was recovery—having something unexpected happen and doing my very best to handle it gracefully and not eating over it. I didn't have much practice at that.

Walking back to the hotel after dinner, I wanted to dance and throw my arms in the air and scream, "Hallelujah!" I didn't do it because . . . well, I was evolved enough that I cared a bit what New Yorkers thought about people crossing their streets.

When I finally started abstaining from sugar, grains, and carbs, I was encouraged to have a quiet time each morning, a time to reconnect with my deeper self—what Quakers call "the still, small voice within." A time to teach myself how to be grateful for what I had instead of miserably focusing on what I didn't have. I felt like I had a leg up on this practice because of my Quaker background.

I started by doing the same things I had done in camp: finding other people's words to express what I was feeling until I could express them myself. I learned some prayers and changed some words so that I felt comfortable and sincere in saying them. As each day passed, I realized that I had been given a huge gift. I had been given freedom from compulsively eating. I was no longer a practicing food addict, I was a recovering food addict. I thought of myself as a pickle who could never become a cucumber again: it was important that I remembered that the disease was arrested, but I would never be cured.

As it turns out, I don't want to be cured. What I have today, because this disease forced my hand in so many ways, is richer than anything I could have planned for or predicted.

Do I ever think about bingeing anymore? Not really. Do I ever think about putting something in my mouth that contains sugar, carbs, or grains? Yes, once in a while. So far, it has remained merely a thought. Usually it's a fleeting thought. Sometimes I know I could just reach out my hand and throw the last fifteen years away. At times like those—when I'm tired or have gone too long without eating and don't want to wait to make a meal—I realize how easy it is to just plain screw up.

This scares me. It scares me enough that I stay very involved with our group. I talk to people who are brand-new and tell them my story. I tell them that I used to eat over every discomfort I ever had, every angry thought and every resentment I nurtured.

Another favorite aphorism of mine is: "Resentment is like swallowing poison and hoping the other person dies." I want to remember what my old life was like because memory is a tricky thing. It can trick me into thinking it wasn't really that bad. I know because I have watched other people start taking their recovery for granted and the next thing I know, they have binged and gone back to a "hell on earth."

I've learned to ask for help—and that doing so doesn't make me weak or stupid. A teacher of mine once said, "The only stupid question is the one you don't ask." I need all the help I can get. Trying to figure out my weight/food problem by myself got me fat and suicidal. If I had had the answers, I certainly would have used them. The addict's mind is very creative. I can have sensible information and still think, *this time it will be different.* If I want to learn about arresting my food addiction, I had to go to the experts and ask for help. But the experts were not doctors or therapists who could only guess what it was like to live in food hell. The experts were the recovering food addicts that made themselves available at all hours of the day to help me. No one who has experienced that insane misery wants to see another person live in it.

Now I'm one of the people who can reach out and say, "No one has to live in food hell ever again. Come do what I do and you'll have what I have. Freedom from compulsively eating and a life to live as other non-addicts live. A life you couldn't dream was possible when you lay on your bed crying because you couldn't stop eating. This is a guarantee."

As the founders of Alcoholics Anonymous so elegantly said:
"It works, it really does[6]."

And what about the relationship with my mother? She was nine-ty-two years old in 2005 when she told me never to return to her home again. The next time I had any communication with her, she didn't remember she had ever said those words to me. I wanted to forgive her; the twelve-step program tells us that with forgiveness comes contentment. But I couldn't let go of the hurt. It was just one more brick on the mountain of painful things she had thrown at me all my life. Even so, I decided I didn't need to *act* the way I felt. In the past, when similar instances occurred, I cut off communication and waited for her to apologize to me. That never happened, and I slowly let her back into my life until the next hurt.

By 2005, somewhere inside of me, I'd begun to accept that my mother was never going to change. So until she died in September of 2008, I continued to visit her three times a year. I never stayed more than four days. That seemed to be the limit of time that either of us could be civil to each other. I was jealous of the relationship my sister seemed to have with her, but I later learned that my jealousy was misplaced. Vicki had her own problems with our mother.

In September 2008, I received a phone call from Anna. She told me that my mother was dying, and I should come right away. The news made me numb, and I waited two days before I flew to Philadelphia. By that time, she was in a coma and all I could do was wait. I kept myself from feeling anything by watching the Philadelphia Phillies win the American League East pennant and head to the World Series.

My mom died three days after I arrived at Pennswood. Then I

---

6   Alcoholics Anonymous, 1939, p.88

transitioned into a mode I was comfortable with: cleaning up the room on the skilled nursing floor where she had lived for the last two years of her life, and organizing her belongings, getting rid of things, and making decisions about what to save. I had made a friend in the Greysheet community in Bucks County, and she invited me to stay in her home as long as I needed. I stayed a month, organized a memorial service for my mother, and patted myself on the back for being such a good daughter. One day, my friend began to tell me how much she admired my mother and everything she had done in her life. I wanted to scream at her, tell her how awful my mother was. I didn't, but I was furious. I felt betrayed by my friend—felt that she had chosen my mother over me.

People weren't blind to the relationship I had with my mother. She had lived at Pennswood twenty years by the time she died. I had come to know many of her friends over the years. At the luncheon after the memorial service, one of the them turned to me and said, "You're free now. You can go live your life." I thought I would cry. She, and probably others, had seen the way my mother treated me, and she seemed to be saying, "It wasn't our place to say anything but we did see how she treated you. Now go have a life."

My mother donated her body to scientific research, and I requested that her ashes be sent to me in California when whatever they did was finished. The box arrived about six months after I returned to Oakland. I kept saying I was going to sprinkle the ashes somewhere, but the box stayed up on a shelf in my closet, going nowhere.

In 2016, I was sitting in a twelve-step meeting and someone was sharing about her relationship with her mother. I have no memory of what she said, but suddenly I had a vision of what it must have been like to have me as a daughter: a fat, rageful, depressed girl who demanded all the attention in the family, spun through everyone's life like a hurricane, and sucked all the air out of a room. I was horrified at the image. I'm not excusing my mother for her lack of parenting skills or her lack of desire to learn how to be a better mother. But it was the first time I'd glimpsed my part in our relationship. Neither one of us had ever forgiven the other for being the way we were.

Later that summer, I was able to take down the box of ashes, put a photo of my beautiful mother in her late thirties in front of the box, and say I was sorry. And I was. I was sorry that food addiction sucks the life out of families, makes enemies of people who could possibly be friends, and destroys everything good in its path.

Somehow, just going through that exercise has relieved me of all the anger, sorrow, and incomprehension I'd lived with all my life until then. I don't miss my mother, but I don't hate her anymore. And I never could have let go of all that "crap" if I had the poison of sugar, grains, and carbohydrates in my body.

I don't know why our lives turn out the way they do, but I'm very sure I'm not the only one with a mother story that isn't pretty. Today, I can talk about it with others and give other people hope that things really can heal. We just have no idea what the healing will look like.

I've been told that my story is the most precious thing I have and sharing it with others can help both me and others not to feel so alone in this world. Life is hard. I have a disease known as food addiction. This is a disease that has a solution. Today, I live in the solution. I feel contented most of the time. I feel happy and joyful much of the time. I feel free all the time: free of the compulsion to put poison in my body, free of the compulsion to self-destruct on a daily basis. I am one of the fortunate ones.

Acknowledgments

It's true that no book gets written by one person. It's hard work and 'takes a village'. My precious village includes April Eberhardt, who read a ten-page vignette and encouraged me to write a memoir; Brooke Warner, who drew out from within me the ability to turn a voice into something readable on paper; my first readers: Leigh, Grainne, Darcy, Peggy, Eileen, Wendy, and Claire; the many people who heard snippets and chapters of this book and told me to keep writing—you know who you are; my mother, who provided the funds that allowed me to be coached for two years. To the thousands of people in recovery from an addiction who showed me, by the power of their example, that I did not have to understand why a solution worked to know it worked: to you I owe my life; my dear friend, Sally Duncan, without whom there may never have been a program of Greysheeters Anonymous; and to my sister who took me to my first Greysheet meeting.

The only way I know how to repay all of you is to pass this message on.

Appendix

To reach Greysheeters Anonymous:

In the United States and Canada
www.greysheet.org
email an area contact, or register for Phone List.
For more information, write: greysheet@greysheet.org
     or phone: 832-856-1058
GSA World Services or GSAWS, Inc.
Cherokee Station
PO Box 20098
New York, NY 10021-0061

In United Kingdom and Europe
Write: info@greysheeteurope.org
Or: gsaeurope@gmail.com

10 am Saturday Morning Meeting
Hinde Street Methodist Church,
West London Mission
Entrance: 19 Thayer St, W1U 2Q
Nearest underground railway station is Bond Street, reached on Central

& Jubilee Lines. Take James' Street, off Oxford Street, walk three blocks, Church on right hand side, corner Thayer & Hinde Streets.

In Israel
http://greysheet.org.il
English speaking: e-mail: gsisraelrbs@gmail.com

In Iceland
www.gsa.is
gsa@gsa.is

GSA is growing in Ireland, Scotland, Belgium, France, Spain, The Netherlands, Germany, Slovakia (see below), Slovenia, Bulgaria (see below), and Sweden. There are also meetings in South Africa and Australia. To reach people in any of these countries, go to the website: www.greysheet.org and look under International contacts. You can also write to the European Intergroup at: gsaeurope@gmail.com

In Bulgaria
Write to: gsabulgaria@gmail.com

In Slovakia
Go to: www.greysheet.weebly.com

To follow Sara Somers and this book:
Instagram: @savingsarathebook
www.sarasomers.com
www.saving-sara.org
Facebook: Saving Sara the book

About the Author

© Henrietta Richer

Sara Somers suffered from active food addiction from age nine to age fifty-eight; she has been in food recovery since 2005. In a double life of sorts, Somers worked as a licensed psychotherapist in the San Francisco Bay Area for thirty-four years. After finding recovery, Somers moved to Paris, France, where she currently lives. She writes a blog called *Out My Window: My Life in Paris*. When she's not writing, Somers volunteers at the American Library in Paris, enjoys the cinema, reads prolifically, and follows her favorite baseball team, the Oakland Athletics. Most important, Somers devotes time each day to getting the word out about food addiction and helping other food addicts. *Saving Sara* is her first book.

SELECTED TITLES FROM SHE WRITES PRESS

She Writes Press is an independent publishing company founded to serve women writers everywhere. Visit us at www.shewritespress.com.

Being Ana: A Memoir of Anorexia Nervosa by Shani Raviv
$16.95, 978-1631521393
In this fast-paced coming-of-age story, Raviv, spirals into anorexia as a misfit fourteen-year-old and spends the next ten years being "Ana" (as many anorexics call it)—until she finally faces the rude awakening that if she doesn't slow down, break her denial, and seek help, she will starve to death.

Learning to Eat Along the Way by Margaret Bendet
$16.95, 978-1-63152-997-9
After interviewing an Indian holy man, newspaper reporter Margaret Bendet follows him in pursuit of enlightenment and ends up facing demons that were inside her all along.

A Different Kind of Same: A Memoir by Kelley Clink
$16.95, 978-1-63152-999-3
Several years before Kelley Clink's brother hanged himself, she attempted suicide by overdose. In the aftermath of his death, she traces the evolution of both their illnesses, and wonders: If he couldn't make it, what hope is there for her?

Where Have I Been All My Life? A Journey Toward Love and Wholeness by Cheryl Rice $16.95, 978-1-63152-917-7
Rice's universally relatable story of how her mother's sudden death launched her on a journey into the deepest parts of grief—and, ultimately, toward love and wholeness.

Insatiable: A Memoir of Love Addiction by Shary Hauer
$16.95, 978-1-63152-982-5
An intimate and illuminating account of corporate executive—and secret love addict—Shary Hauer's migration from destructive to healthy love.

Blinded by Hope: One Mother's Journey Through Her Son's Bipolar Illness and Addiction by Meg McGuire $16.95, 978-1-63152-125-6
A fiercely candid memoir about one mother's roller coaster ride through doubt and denial as she attempts to save her son from substance abuse and bipolar illness.

Printed in the United States
by Baker & Taylor Publisher Services